How to Read the World:
Creation in Evolution

Christian Montenat, Luc Plateaux
and Pascal Roux

How to Read the World:
Creation in Evolution

SCM PRESS LTD

Translated by John Bowden from the French
Pour lire la Création dans l'Évolution
published 1984 by Les Editions du Cerf,
29 bd Latour-Maubourg, Paris

Nihil obstat: Anton Cowan
            Censor
Imprimatur: Rt Revd Mgr John Crowley, VG
            Westminster
            13 June 1985

The *Nihil obstat* and *Imprimatur* are a declaration that a book or
pamphlet is considered to be free from doctrinal or moral error. It
is not implied that those who have granted the *Nihil obstat* and
Imprimatur agree with the contents, opinions or statements
expressed.

British Library Cataloguing in Publication Data
Monterrat, Christian
    How to read the world: creation in evolution.
    1. Creation   2. Evolution—Religious aspects
    —Christianity
    I. Title   II. Plateaux, Luc   III. Roux, Pascal
    IV. Pour lire la création dans l' évolution. *English*
    231.7'65   BS651

ISBN 0–334–02053–0

334 02053 0

First published in English 1985
by SCM Press Ltd, 26-30 Tottenham Road, London N1

Typeset at The Spartan Press Ltd, Lymington, Hants
and printed in Great Britain by Fletcher & Son Ltd, Norwich

Contents

Though the texts have been read and criticized by the group, they were written by those whose names stand against each chapter.

Contents of Boxes

Preface

This book has been produced by an inter-disciplinary group which met monthly over several years. The group was made up of a priest (Pascal Roux) with scientific training and scientists who were Christians. A geologist (Christian Montenat) and a biologist (Luc Plateaux) were also joined by an ethologist (J. -P. Signoret) and a paleontologist (M. Godinot), who attended less regularly, though their contributions were no less valuable. Each chapter has been written (or inspired) by one or two authors, whose names are given on the Contents page; however, all the book has been read and discussed by all the group. This method has led to variations in style between one chapter and another; similarly, differences of tone or perspective reflect the fact that each of the authors is implicitly addressing a certain kind of audience.

This book is not a treatise of Christian faith, nor is it a philosophical, biological or palaeontological study. Obviously it does not tell the whole story: while we have tried to be as exact and as precise as possible, we are aware of the limits of our enterprise and of our own capacities. Our aim has been to mark out a meeting place, to draw views together, to indicate topics for reflection, and to show the possibility of and the need for harmony between faith and objective scientific knowledge in the sphere of biological evolution, which is so fraught with controversy. We think that there is an urgent need to demonstrate how evolution, seen in faith, expresses the history of creation. We are not the first to attempt this, and we shall be happy if we stimulate deeper thinking about some of the questions that we raise. There is much here which ought to be taken up and discussed at greater depth by others with more expertise.

Today, human thought is constantly on the move, as it has been since ancient times. That is why in some instances it has often seemed to us proper to follow up several trains of thought, regardless of whether all of us, or some of us, prefer one particular view. Others may legitimately continue to be doubtful where we are convinced. It is less legitimate to reject outright, as being utterly wrong, what gives hundreds of millions of people their reason for living.

Given the subject matter, we often use the language of faith: we do not mean to mislead readers who are not believers, but to express in simple terms the intellectual coherence at which believers need to aim. We have thought very carefully about those of our readers who do not share our faith but who want to join in our investigation of the origin of life, the stages of hominization, and our philosophical and theological reflection on an overall interpretation of life, of human beings and their ultimate future. Thank you for reading this book. We would welcome any criticisms, suggestions or remarks which could help us to make it more profound. We hope that you will find that we have respected your sincerity and your differences. Our prime concern has been to establish some new links between those who, while not knowing one another, are nevertheless members of the same humanity, even if they do not share our deepest and dearest convictions.

Evolution and Creation

Although other ideas may have been put forward down the centuries, for humanity generally the predominant opinion has long been that the living world owes its origin to an instantaneous creation. This notion was supported by the idea, prevalent among scientists down to the end of the eighteenth century, that the species were fixed. Such a notion was easily arrived at by simply observing successive generations of beings apparently similar to their ancestors, which must necessarily have derived from an original filiation.

Religions have had, and still have, different interpretations of an original creation. Genesis gives us an interpretation centred on the one Creator, source of all existence and all life; all known beings proceed from the creative will of this Creator. They are classified in a certain order, depending on the degree of their perfection, whether greater or lesser. The appearance of instantaneous creation given by the narrative partly derives from a concern to associate each form of existence directly with the action of the Creator; the nature of the creative process is alien

Creationism

From the beginnings of history, human cultures have handed down to us ideas about the origin of humanity and the origin of the world around us. This origin is always associated with one or more beings endowed with great power. These beings give existence to what men and women discover, with considerable wonderment, to be achievements far beyond their own powers of realization.

In the lifetime of an individual human being, nature could seem to be immutable. Everything that the individual saw coming into being resembled that which gave it birth. This naturally led to the idea of an instantaneous beginning, the date of which in earlier times used to be pushed back to that of the earliest ancestors who could be conjured up by a memory which often idealized them.

The affirmation of one, universal God would seem to be the distinctive mark of the people of Israel. We find a similar affirmation in Egypt round about the time that Israel came into being (with the Pharaoh Akhenaten). Such a God cannot but be the sole Creator of all there is, and reflection on creation – on the beginnings of the world – developed among the wise men of Israel, some centuries after its birth as a nation. (Originally, in a pre-reflective stage, it had no culture other than its nomadic life and the heritage of faith in its God.) This reflection necessarily borrowed from neighbouring civilizations the idea that the world came about as the result of creation by superior beings; however, it bore the original stamp of Israel. The idea of multiple rival creators or demiurges (sub-creators) was corrected by the assertion that there was only one God who had created all things. That gave creation a coherence which polytheistic conceptions lacked. The affirmation of the omnipotence of the Creator whose word is obeyed without delay ('God said . . . and it was done') tends to reinforce the impression of the instantaneous character of creation.

Despite some ancient and often unfounded reflections on the possible transformation of living forms, for a long time the idea of evolution remained alien to humanity. Ideas about the origin of the world and mankind were expressed in terms of different 'creationisms', i.e. in arguments for the existence of an original creation in various forms.

A Christianized creationism dominated the West in the eighteenth and nineteenth centuries, when ideas about transformation developed. Since at that time it was mixed up with a divine revelation, the form of which seemed as intangible as its basis, this creationism was defended with the passion people reserve for safeguarding whatever they hold most precious and most dear. That led to intolerance. However, not all the creationists were Christians, as is evident, say, from Voltaire's attachment to this conception.

The evidence of the differences between the successive forms observed by geologists in 'antediluvian' strata suggested that in the course of time numerous creations were replaced. Thus d'Orbigny proposed twenty-seven consecutive creations. This creationism by repetition was the argument used by opponents of the transformists, who argued for the transformation of species from the change in geological fauna.

Creationism went into decline when the fossil series made a continuous evolution more probable, and similarly, the study of living species demonstrated kindred features, probably indicating descent from common ancestors. However, there are those who accept evolution as an explanation of the living world, while reserving for humanity a special creation enabling men and women to be distinguished from the animal world. This concern to put human beings outside the animal world still governs the attachment of some people to creationism, whether in connection with the world as a whole or at least in connection with human beings. This creationism is often associated with a very literal interpretation of biblical terms (called fundamentalism, see p. 88). It is no longer professed by a number of Christian churches, which recognize, implicitly or explicitly (*Humani generis*, 1950), the possibility of an evolution leading up to the human race.

That in no way implies that Christians no longer affirm their belief in a creation. The idea of creation must not be confused with creationist theory. It is quite possible to profess faith in a God who is Creator of all things without concluding that creation is instantaneous. The idea of creation has now been permeated by the historical perspective which has left its stamp on all the Bible (it is now seen as the history of the actions and words of God for humanity): thus it is commonplace for Christian believers to see creation as a permanent action of the Creator, the history of which is described by evolution.

to the preoccupations of the authors of Genesis.

The philosophical and religious disputes in the nineteenth century crystallized in the view that creation and evolution were in conflict: creation was understood only in terms of the instantaneous realization of the will of the Creator (and the idea of creation was reduced to those terms). Nowadays we find that some Christians who still accept this understanding of creation are forced back into a position where they have either to reject particular scientific discoveries or to renounce their faith.

However, this conflict between creation and evolution has considerably diminished among Christians, and not just among those with specialist training, because they meet fellow-Christians claiming that there is harmony between creation and evolution. Nevertheless, the conflict between creation and evolution remains an obstacle to evangelization, essentially because it persists so tenaciously in the minds of those who are not believers. These people have never had to ask this question from the perspective of faith (or have answered it only superficially, in the negative), and they often continue to associate Christianity inextricably with a creationism which they reject in its entirety; such confusion is often encouraged by the media and in education and popular discussion.

Now this reduction of creation to an instantaneous creationism has never been characteristic of the way theologians have thought about the Creator and his creation (the church fathers, St Thomas Aquinas, etc., and even some of the Psalms). It is above all the result of too literal a reading of biblical imagery. The Creator is not only the one who acts at the first point in time, but the Being whose creative will gives existence to all being at every moment. He is the Being who guides the history of the universe and human history, not necessarily by specific and repeated interventions, but already and above all by the existence that he gives and sustains in his creative will, in accordance with the modes of being which he determines. These modes are not subject to the caprices of the Creator, since he remains faithful to the final goal for which he has ordained his creation; so it is that he presents us with an intelligible world as a first step towards knowing him.

That is why the Christian need not be afraid of finding a contradiction between creation and the Creator. On the contrary, the rationality of the creation reflects the intellect of the Creator. This creation is to be accepted as the first form of language in which God addresses those whom he has created, as a kind of pre-revelation addressed to all human beings, but one which can be misunderstood or travestied by them. Moreover, when the sciences allow us to be quite certain about some of their discoveries, we must not be afraid to say that these discoveries can illuminate our faith. For example, they can help us to distinguish in the messages about God handed down to us by our ancestors between what is part of the cultural expression of an epoch or a country and the essential word of God. These new realities can also stimulate this faith, bringing it new knowledge to penetrate.

Science is alienating if it is approached as a self-sufficient totality which claims to say all that can be said about humanity; however, the true scientist recognizes the limits to scientific method. Similarly, one can only approach faith properly by keeping free of all practical or theoretical absolutism.

The Christian who is already familiar with the presence of God in history can envisage biological evolution, and similarly the evolution of the universe, as the overall way in which creation unfolds. This conception is not new (it was already put forward by Pierre Teilhard de Chardin and Karl Rahner), though at present it is largely unknown, above all to those who are not believers, and even to some believers. Such ignorance is both an obstacle to the evangelization of the former and a handicap to the faith of the latter. The vital thing is that those in authority should make a pronouncement on how faith can be strengthened and nurtured in an evolutionary view of creation. If the authorities still need evidence, this book is ours.

Culture and Faith:
A Barrier or a Springboard?

Louis Dufréty, a friend of Bernanos' 'country priest', explained that his intellectual development had estranged him from the faith. This attitude is not just the novelist's own construction. We can often see a conflict between 'the man of reason' and 'the man of faith', and I know more than one student who has justified his rejection of the faith by his intellectual maturity. Indeed some, like Louis Dufréty, have been 'convinced' and active Christians up to the day when, confronted with a certain intellectual experience which they have been unable to integrate into their faith, they have rejected their faith as being a strait-jacket. I can remember a group of intelligent students in which many 'lost their faith'. And I think of a remark by one of them, who said to me, 'Oh, we're past that sort of thing.'

Christians are disturbed at this sort of attitude. If so many people 'lose their faith' as they acquire a broader education, is not this education the basic trouble? Are not all human efforts to know and understand the created world vain and ridiculous? That might seem to be the case, since these efforts alienate people from the Author of what has been made. He is the only one who can explain everything and help us to understand his works. The problem is that so many people get lost in the name of their intellectual pretensions. Does that mean that we have to renounce all intellectual claims? Why not? 'If your eye offends you . . .'

Offends you about what? If some people have not succeeded in integrating their intellectual develop-ment into their faith, is this not rather because their faith was too narrow? Perhaps their God was too small? Whether because of a narrow-minded educa-tion or through laziness – the laziness of a faith which has never had to struggle – have they not reduced God to their level, as an imaginary and familiar being, dressed in every-day clothes? And when the time came to change, they cast off God along with their old skin. They made God in their own size, and when they grew, instead of enlarging their faith beyond its present limits, they made God a thing of the past.

Now we are all tempted to make God in our image. The Jewish people told us this long ago, as they struggled with the laziness of a faith which hesitated between the living God and the desire for an image which provided a resting place. However, faith only lives if it progresses. Who can boast of having a conception of God which matches reality? Surely we always have something to discover! No matter how much we broaden our horizons, God is always beyond them: 'I am the one who is beyond your imagining.' We build up our lives on intellectual values and use them to look for God, each on his or her own territory. Philosophers may cross-question their arguments, scientists may push their science to the limits, others may discover vast tracts of unknown territory – yet God is beyond it all! Do we not have a powerful springboard for our faith here, at the heart of our lives? And beyond the specializations, however vast our culture, however great our awareness of the world around us; the more that we explore, the more we discover how much we have to learn, the more we become aware of the Infinite which will always be beyond our grasp. We shall escape the insidious temptation of thinking that we know it all: we shall see how much God is beyond us. I remember an aunt of mine who helped those with incurable diseases to turn to God. She would present them with an astronomical panorama, expecting that the vastness of the distances involved and of the stars would stagger them! One is tempted to smile . . . : they believed in the stars and not in God. But who knows? The stars took them out of themselves, so that they could encounter God, authentically, a God who went beyond them, who was not in their image, who was not as they had first imagined him.

Far from being an obstacle to faith, some education can even help people to faith, provided that it is 'open', i.e. directed towards what has still to be discovered and above all towards what can be attained; for if we only contemplate what we know, what we have attained, how do we discover that which has no limit? This is true of all our concerns: whatever human beings derive from themselves leaves them the same. However, sooner or later, God manifests himself to all those who are open, if only by one of his greatest manifestations of himself among us: the faith which he puts in us, the faith of his church, faith in his word. For if God is beyond us, only revelation will allow us to discover him.

We would like to be able to say something to those who, whether or not they are believers, are trying to understand how the scientific facts of evolution change the external framework of revelation without altering its essential content. With such an understanding, these facts, which are part of present-day culture, could help us to live in the faith, just as elements of Christianized cultures have always helped Christians in the past. We know that acts of faith cannot be forced as a result of reasoning; they can only be invited. We also know that it is dangerous to make too direct connections between the divine Absolute and imperfect, sometimes transitory, knowledge which risks dragging down faith with it when it is changed or disappears. However, faith is alive here and now, not outside time and space; it is called on to penetrate and illuminate all culture, including modern scientific culture. This is why, without claiming to use science for apologetic ends, we are right to show that our faith can be supported by our scientific knowledge, as it can rely on everything that we receive from God.

Chapter 1 gives a brief account of the characteristics of living matter, showing its extreme complexity in comparison with inert matter. In spite of that, we can envisage how living matter will have grown out of inert matter, a genesis the stages of which are described as events which would seem to be predetermined rather than chance. This blurs the divisions between biology and chemistry, physics and mathematics. Christians can see this new perspective as a unification of creation, growing out of a coherent creative will and directed towards its Creator.

In Chapter 2 we look at the palaeontological history of living beings. This shows us how they progress towards increasing autonomy, depending on the extent of their evolution; those that are 'most evolved' progressively escape from all the conditions which gave them birth, thus arriving at a threshold of freedom.

Chapter 3, based on a comparative description of animal behaviour, specifies the stages by which behaviour can reach such a threshold of freedom. This leads to definitions of the characteristics of true freedom (long-term planning, self-determination, shaping of individual behaviour), showing how human beings achieve this freedom and how they can fail to achieve it.

Chapter 4 deals with hominization. First it reminds us of what we know from palaeontological discoveries and what these tell us about development and activities leading up to man. We next establish the point at which human beings took shape 'anatomically'; then, on the basis of characteristics of behaviour (long-term planning, innovation, transmission of techniques), we try to establish the point at which 'metaphysical' man came into being. So this chapter is concerned with questions about the cradle of humanity, whether human beings have descended from a single pair or from more (monogenism or polygenism), and the discontinuity or continuity of hominization.

Chapter 5 first raises the question inevitably associated with any reading of Genesis, 'What is man?' This question concerns everyone, whether or not they are believers. The chapter then describes the circumstances in which the first chapters of Genesis were written, circumstances which to some degree shaped the imagery of the story. Lastly, it shows how these chapters form a theological and anthropological synthesis, composed in a mythical style aimed at communicating the inexpressible by images drawn from specific experience and with a preexisting cultural basis. Thus to say that originally there was only one human couple would seem above all to be an affirmation of the unity of humanity, rather than of historic fact.

Chapter 6 begins by raising the problem of evil, which forces itself on everyone in every age. Then it considers this problem in the light of the new covenant in Christ , whose word reveals to us the existence of the 'father of lies' and tells us that 'in the beginning' men and women neither rejected nor broke with each other. Christ, faced with evil and death, claims to be the resurrection and the life and proves this by his own resurrection. The chapter shows that original sin is essentially a matter of human beings claiming the status of God and appropriating the knowledge of good and evil (and deciding between them). The divorce between human beings and God brings them up against the existential drama of their death, which no longer has the character of a journey to God.

Chapter 7 tries to raise the question of the role of evolution in its three dimensions: biological, cultural and spiritual. Beginning from reflection on the tension between the infinite desire of humanity and our limits in space and time, it opens up the horizons of an act of faith in a creator God who, in Jesus Christ, transforms biological death into a definitive passage towards eternal life.

Belief in God the Creator

Is it not naive or rash to believe that this world is the work of a Creator concerned for our good? The experience shared by men and women hardly suggests that everything has been disposed 'with wisdom and in love'. However, without hesitation, we affirm his providence, professing our hope for the end of time. This hope will not be disappointed, for its guarantee is the love of our God for this creation, whose limitations and sufferings he was willing to share in the incarnation of his Son. Therefore to speak of the Creator is not to shut God up in the past, but to affirm a living relationship with him in the present. To speak of the Creator is also to look towards the future, since the creative act is a loving call which invites us all to shape our lives and all humanity to live out its history in response to this call. For God, who creates humanity in a marvellous way and who renews it even more wondrously in Jesus Christ, will give us 'glory and splendour' in full measure (cf.Ps.8.6) when the new heavens and the new earth appear.

So, here and for the future, affirming our faith in the Creator, we offer an answer to the questions which are engraved on the conscience of the human race. On earth we are not alone; we do not find ourselves here by chance or by mistake; we are not unwanted. The scientific understanding of this world and its technological transformation still leave us facing the deepest mystery. What is the meaning of life? Towards what destiny are we bound?

We believe that God's design is to bring all human beings together in his well-beloved Son. For 'all things have been created by him and in him', 'everything subsists in him', 'in him all things have been created, visible and invisible' (Col.1.17,16). As Christians, we believe that God the Father has created all things by his Son, eternal wisdom, word of life, light for humanity.

The Bishops of France

1

The Origin of Life

The Problem of the Origin of Life

I believe that if we are to respect the many implications of the origin of life and to avoid reducing it to one particular area – whether science, philosophy or religion – we must consider it simultaneously from a scientific, a philosophical and a religious perspective.

Joël de Rosnay, *Les Origines de la Vie*

The living being

It is impossible to talk about the appearance of life without giving a more precise definition of life or, more exactly, of living beings. Living beings are primarily defined by their extremely complex structure. We know that new properties appear in every complex system which are properties only of the whole system and cannot be reduced to the sum of the properties of the individual parts. Thus every molecule has new properties which are not those of any of the atoms which make it up; the same is true of macromolecules as compared with the simple molecules of which they are made up, of the cell with regard to the macromolecules which it contains, and of multicellular entities with regard to their component cells. Transition to the next level calls for the input of energy in a particular environment, and is possible only in certain conditions. This determines the character of developments from simple forms to complex forms; the existence of living beings and our geological knowledge shows that these developments have proved possible on earth.

It is not enough to define the living being in terms of complexity of structure. The living being has certain essential features: constant movement – and renewal – of matter and energy to ensure the formation and maintenance of the structure which is its necessary frame (though the structure may sometimes be dormant, it cannot remain so indefinitely). This structure and internal movement are controlled by a complex programme of information incorporated into the structure (the genetic code). So the living being is permeated by a flux of matter and energy; it is maintained by its organization, its 'form'.

By this permanent internal movement the living being provides for its needs, forms its own components, grows, multiplies, reproduces itself, engenders other living beings which with it form a group (a 'species') that evolves. Endowed with both an internal and an external activity of its own, the living being can be considered an active subject in its environment.

The most obvious thing about this living being is its individuality. It forms a totality enclosed within an external surface which separates it from its environment. It provides for its support by taking in food which it transforms and incorporates into its organism. Maintaining itself calls for an input of energy which the living being obtains by consuming part of its food. All this calls for constant internal movement which brings about a chemical mixing of the elements involved. This movement also uses up energy; it can remain internal to the living being, but it can also manifest itself externally by the movements of this living being. So the living being also acquires another potential: autonomous move-

ment, one of the features which distinguish animals from vegetables. When all movement ceases, it often means that the living being is dead. However, there are forms of 'retarded' or 'dormant' life, of such a kind that the living structure can maintain itself without any movement, without actually dying and without changing. So what characterizes life is the possibility of resuming movement in favourable conditions. If this possibility no longer exists, the organism is dead. Thus movement and the flux of matter remain essential, even if they are only potential.

The living being is further defined by its capacity to build itself up through growth, and to reproduce itself once it has grown, thus propagating life. This propagation of life is not stagnant in the forms that it assumes; these forms are not immutable over periods of geological time. One can see great differences between the living beings of one geological age and the next, but there is an apparent continuity in the variation. The living being evolves; as far as it is concerned, that is another form of movement, an overall movement which gives successive generations their place in an evolutionary dynamic.

Finally, none of this could come about without the necessary coordination of all the reactions involved; within the living being, functions are constantly regulated.

Thus Joël de Rosnay is led to define the three basic functions of living beings as self-conservation, self-reproduction and self-regulation. The dynamism of the living being lies essentially in its reproduction of itself, based on the way in which it builds itself up (self-construction), so we shall devote most of our attention to that.

However, before we do so, we ought to have some idea of the orders of magnitude of the elements that we shall be considering. Figure 1 gives us a logarithmic scale of dimensions. It shows how much our knowledge of living matter owes to techniques of microscopic observation, which have developed only over the last three centuries.

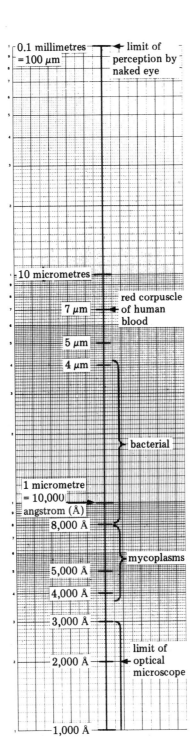

Figure 1 **Logarithmic scale of the dimensions of the elements of living matter.**
The upper limit of the scale is the smallest length perceptible to the naked eye: a tenth of a millimetre, equivalent to 100 micrometres (or microns), the micrometre (m) itself amounting to 10,000 angström (Å). The scale shows us the dimensions of bacteria (and mycoplasms), viruses, large proteins, and the limits of perception (the capacity to separate) of the optical microscope and the electronic microscope. The lower limit of the scale is the size of a molecule of water.

0.1 millimetres = 100 μm ← limit of perception by naked eye

10 micrometres

7 μm ← red corpuscle of human blood

5 μm

4 μm

bacterial

1 micrometre = 10,000 angstrom (Å)

8,000 Å

mycoplasms

5,000 Å

4,000 Å

3,000 Å

2,000 Å ← limit of optical microscope

1,000 Å

1,000 Å

virus

200 Å

100 Å

80 Å

proteins

10 Å

5 Å ← limits of electron microscope

1 Å ← molecule of water

How living matter forms and reproduces itself

All living beings are made up of a collection of chemical substances of which water is the most abundant. Other substances play a part in the formation of living matter: sugars and fats (lipids) are the indispensable elements, but often have the most passive role. The nucleic acids (RNA and DNA) and the proteins are the essentials in the functioning and the formation of living organisms, and play an active part in the mechanisms by which they are constructed. The way in which they function determines the development of all the other elements. The proteins, controlled by the nucleic acids, which determine the programmes of synthesis, form the active elements in living cells. Certain proteins perform a supportive role (as a skeleton or protection), and others help to form pores in membranes, but the most important proteins are those which constantly act as catalysts for chemical reactions in the living being: the enzymes.

All these proteins are made up of an assembly of elementary 'bricks', the amino-acids, brought together in a precise order to form a protein chain: this chain folds in on itself and consolidates itself by 'bridges' constructed between certain atoms in such a way as to take on the characteristic form of the macromolecule which it constitutes, a form adapted to a precise function. Only a few amino-acids (about twenty) are involved in the construction of proteins (see Figure 2).

Figure 2

Diagram of a fragment of the amino-acid chain, the extremities of which show the ions OH− and H+. These interact during the addition of a new amino-acid: the two ions join up to form a molecule of water. This results in a -CO-NH- link (peptide link) which attaches the new amino-acid to the chain. Of course the chain in no way forms a straight line.

The shaded parts are a simplified representation of the hydrophobic parts of each amino-acid. Here we see only eight of the twenty L alpha amino-acids on living matter: glycine, alanine, valine, leucine, isoleucine, proline, phenylalanine, tyrosine, typtophan, lysine, arginine, histidine, serine, threonine, cysteine, methionine, asparagine, glutamine, aspartic acid, glutamic acid.

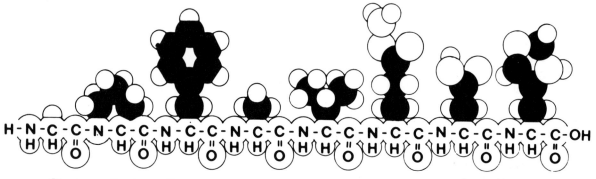

Glycine   Proline   Phenylalanine   Alanine   Valine   Glutamine   Aspartic Acid   Histidine

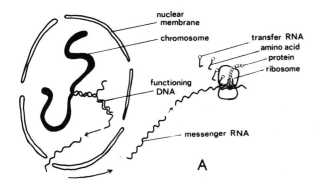

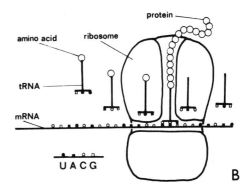

nuclear membrane
chromosome
transfer RNA
amino acid
protein
ribosome
functioning DNA
messenger RNA

A

protein
amino acid
ribosome
tRNA
mRNA

U A C G

B

The assembly of amino-acids and proteins takes place in the structures within cells, called ribosomes, which are themselves made up of ribonucleic acid (RNA) and proteins. The assembly programme is brought to the surface of the ribosome by a long messenger chain of RNA molecules, synthesized in the nucleus of the cell on the basis of the programme of another molecule chain, deoxyribonucleic acid (DNA, Figure 3). The synthesis always takes place in the living cell, which can come in two basic types. Because it is more primitive, the first type is called procaryotic: its cell wall encloses cytoplasm, a liquid medium containing the ribosomes and in which the chromosome is suspended. The chromosome does not in fact have a separate nucleus; one could say that the cell itself is its nucleus. The second type is called eucaryotic. It has an individualized cellular nucleus, separated from the cytoplasm by a membrane, and containing the cellular DNA in the form of chromosomes; by contrast, the ribosomes in the cytoplasm are outside the nucleus.

Thus the nucleus of the cell contains a collection of DNA programmes which control all the syntheses taking place in the cell. This DNA is assembled in the chromosomes, where each

Figure 3
From the DNA programme to the protein
Deoxyribonucleic Acid, DNA, contains a sugar, deoxyribose. Ribonucleic acid, RNA, contains a sugar, ribose.

A. The chromosome is made up of a collection of genes, each of which is a long DNA molecule. The length of chromosomes in most living beings usually seems to be very small because the filaments wrap themselves round in several spirals. However, when a gene is functioning (one example is when DNA programmes a synthesis of messenger RNA), it is always unspiralled and elongated. Messenger RNA (mRNA) leaves the nucleus by a pore in the membrane and enters the cytoplasm, where it is 'deciphered' by a ribosome (see B). Here the mRNA is represented in an elongated form to make things easier to understand, but it actually moves in the form of a cluster.

B. In the course of the 'decipherment' which results in the synthesis of a protein, mRNA unstrings its bases (uracil U, cytosine C, adenine A, guanine G) in the ribosome; each group of three consecutive bases (triplet) forms a recognition signal (codon) which attracts the complementary signal (anticodon) of the transfer RNA (tRNA). Each tRNA carries a characteristic amino-acid of the codon (and the anticodon). The bases which come opposite each other when the anticodon is attached to the codon are always uracile and adenine on the one hand (U-A coupling) and cytosine and guanine on the other (C-G coupling). When the tRNA is in place, its amino-acid fuses with the protein chain, which is thus lengthened by an element. When the mRNA has finished unstringing, the protein chain is synthesized.

23

Figure 4 **Structure and synthesis of DNA**

A. Diagram of the double chain of nucleotides making up DNA. A nucleotide N is made up of a phosphoric acid P, a sugar S, which here is deoxyribose, and a base taken from one of the four following: adenine A, guanine G, thymine T and cytosine C. These bases are the same as those of RNA except for thymine, which replaces uracil. Each chain is made up of a series of links – sugar-acid phosphate bonds. The two chains are bonded by the attraction of bases which always form the same pairs, A-T and G-C; these pairings are determined by the existence of two attracting pairs of atoms in one case and three in the other.

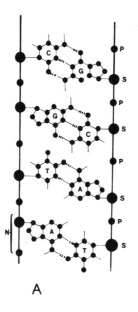

A

B. The double chain of DNA does not really take the form of a straight line, but is twisted into a double helical curve, hence the name double helix which is given to it. This double helix reproduces itself (replication) by opening out; each of the strands then acts as the negative to bring about synthesis with its new complement. An enzyme makes the double helix open; an enzyme is also the catalyst for the synthesis of the strands, by assembling matching elements. When the DNA serves to make the messenger RNA (transcription), the double helix also opens, again under the action of an enzyme; another enzyme catalyzes the assembly of the mRNA, on to which the content of one of the two strands is copied (the other strand is said to be 'silent').

B

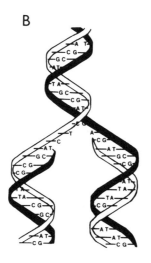

programme for synthesizing a protein constitutes a gene. We are still a long way from knowing how the genes relate to one another and what actual effects they produce in a living being, above all when this being is made up of countless cells. But we know how DNA is made. It is an assembly of two chains of chemical elements held together by forces of attraction, one of the chains being the negative of the other. Moreover, this double chain is twisted on itself in such a way as to form a double helical curve (Figure 4).

The study of these phenomena has been carried out principally on bacteria (procaryotes), but it has been demonstrated that similar phenomena occur in the more complex cells (eucaryotes) of which all animals and vegetables are formed. So the way in which bacteria function is wholly programmed by hundreds of genes (a thousand have been identified in connection with the *E.coli* bacillus). DNA controls the synthesis of RNA which serves to synthesize proteins. So the programme begins with DNA and is carried out through the action of numerous protein enzymes, themselves synthesized by specific genes. Here we have the 'basic dogma' of cellular genetics; according to this the information necessarily goes from the DNA to the RNA and then to the protein; the information can never get back from the result (the protein) to its source (DNA). In 1970 this dogma was, however, partially challenged by work on viruses.

From inert matter to living matter

Is there an important qualitative, irreducible difference between inert matter and living matter? Throughout nature as we know it the answer would seem to be yes, because of the extreme complexity of the structure of living beings and of the hierarchy of their functions under the control of a store of information. The innumerable chemical reactions of living matter are channelled, ordered, by processes very different from the statistical processes of physics. We have seen that for life to exist, very complex and complementary elements are needed in its environment. On the one hand, the nucleic acids need protein enzymes for each of their operations: the transcription of the messenger RNA, the transfer RNA, the replication of DNA and so on; proteins join them to form ribosomes. On the other hand, all the proteins, including the enzymes, are programmed by DNA genes. This would seem to produce a vicious circle: the proteins need nucleic acids, but the nucleic acids cannot subsist without the action of the proteins. Which began the process of autosynthesis, the proteins or the nucleic acids? Was not a quite exceptional initial event needed to produce a first living cell containing nucleic acids and proteins, which could then lead by evolution to other living beings? In fact the world as it is does not seem to contain all the intermediate entities which would substantiate a continuous transition between inert matter and living beings.

Viruses can in fact be supposed to be on the borderline between inert matter and living matter: they have a genetic programme, but not the mechanisms for synthesis and the production of energy which are indispensable to all living beings. They thus have the role of parasites which would seem to be consequent on the existence of living beings. Smaller still are the viroids, molecules of RNA, too short to programme a protein, but which bring about their own manufacture by the cell on which they are parasites. They too would seem to exist as a consequence of the living cell.

To a more elementary degree, certain properties of living beings can be found in inanimate structures. For example, globules rich in organic matter, microdrops (among which de Rosnay includes Oparin's coacervates and Fox's microspheres), form in experimental biochemical 'soups'. These retain a very simple structure (essentially a limiting membrane), absorb organic molecules and even divide, thus multiplying their number. In the case of these properties there does not seem to be an unbridgable gulf between inert matter and living matter. Of course the microdrop can only exploit its own milieu, without itself producing any synthesis of its constituent parts. It represents no more than a first stage in the transition from inert matter to living matter.

So if we are still at a loss confronted with the complexity of living beings and the appearance of this complexity, none of the properties of these beings seems to go beyond the natural consequences of their dynamic complexity and thus to call for a supernatural intervention.

In a more historical perspective, it must of course be noted that we do not know the organization of the first and simplest living beings, nor that of the pre-biological structures which preceded them. These beings evolved in a milieu very different from the present-day ocean, where living beings absorb organic matter and use it to their own advantage. It is certain that the current presence in our world of living beings in a developed state, with their speed of energetic or synthetic reaction, makes it virtually impossible for us to observe the stages of the possible genesis of living beings; these stages will have been removed from the scene by the activities of evolved living beings. Furthermore, it is not at all certain that the genesis of living matter would be possible in conditions on earth as they now are. Scientists are in fact certain that this genesis came about in quite different conditions, and think that the conditions in which we live, particularly the presence of an atmosphere made up of oxygen, make the genesis of life impossible today. One might suppose that the progress of micropalaeontology and of biochemical experimentation will enable us to determine increasingly clearly which hypotheses are possible (who knows whether we may not yet discover elementary living beings or pre-living beings in nature as it is, if not on earth, at least perhaps elsewhere?). Many things have managed to come about slowly, but copiously, given the vast length of geological periods.

From chance to the inevitable

In the past twenty or thirty years, there have been important developments in thinking which have changed theories about the origin of life. There is no longer talk of life having been introduced on earth by a meteorite carrying living germs; that only pushes the problem back one stage further, and in any case is open to very substantial objections (heating of such a meteorite by the atmosphere, and so on). Nor is it any longer supposed that life began from an original cell which appeared by an extraordinary chance or by a special creation. Granted, it is still thought very improbable that life should have appeared on earth, as is evident from Jacques Monod's view: 'The universe was not pregnant with life, nor the biosphere with humanity.' That statement is made in the context of the revival of a theory bringing together chance and necessity.

However, experiments made in conditions more or less similar to those of earth in its primitive state have led, almost unexpectedly, to the spontaneous synthesis of a great many organic compounds of greater or lesser diversity, which we find again specifically in living beings. So much is that the case that many scientists now accept that the appearance of life on earth was not only very probable, but even inevitable, simply because of the interplay of the laws of physics and chemistry. This life had to appear, given the conditions of the primitive earth, and it certainly appeared several times, following a variety of lines. Similarly, the transition from the unicellular to the polycellular stage, which was once thought only to have happened twice (with animals and plants), because it seemed so improbable, has appeared on twelve different lines of descent in recent schemes. The fact that there were many starting points does not mean that living structures were not similar; they seem to have utilized the only possible means of construction. Thus evolution would seem to have been predominantly channelled by the laws of physics, chemistry and biology, with the result that it has proved possible to say, 'The universe *was* pregnant with life.' This theory of the origin of life, which is much more determinist, seems to be winning out over the earlier theory, which is being increasingly abandoned.

The genesis of living systems

It has never proved possible to reconstruct the different stages of the genesis of living matter by a single chain of experiments which demonstrate in continuous succession the transition from inert matter to the living cell. Such an experiment would amount to 'spontaneous generation'. Theories about spontaneous generation were very much in vogue in Pasteur's time. Since people were unaware at that time of the extreme complexity of living matter, these theories simplified the genesis of living beings in a way which now seems to us to be ridiculous. The rigour and precision of Pasteur's work did away with them. So living beings appeared as new creations, lacking any continuity with inert matter.

We now know the importance of the time factor in evolution; researchers studying the genesis of life no longer dream of the almost magical recipe which would produce living beings in a few moments. On the contrary, they try to reconstruct the stages of biogenesis one by one, knowing that each one required a good deal of time, and that several stages took place in a precise order, corresponding to successive different situations, each situation proving favourable to the corresponding stage.

The *first stage* was retraced by the experiments of Stanley Miller in 1953. For a week, this chemist produced electrical discharges in a balloon containing an atmosphere made up of methane (CH_4), water vapour (H_2O), ammonia (NH_3) and hydrogen (H_2). These ingredients represented the atmosphere of primitive earth as suggested by the facts of geology and astrophysics. The circulation of water vapour with condensation drew off the compounds which were able to form

The Abyss of the Past

Marvellous as it is, marvellous as it seems to us in its isolation among the other constructions of matter, the cell, like everything else in the world, cannot be understood (i.e. incorporated into a coherent system of the universe) unless we situate it on an evolutionary line between a past and a future. We have paid a good deal of attention to its development and its differentiations. It is on its origins, that is to say on its roots in the inorganic, that we must now focus our researches if we want to grasp the essence of its novelty. . . *Probing backwards*, we see the cell merging qualitatively and quantitatively with the world of chemical structures. Followed in a backward direction, it visibly converges towards the molecule. . . The discovery of viruses and other similar elements not only adds another and important term to our series of states and forms of matter; it obliges us to interpolate a hitherto forgotten era (an era of sub-life) in the series of ages that measure the past of our planet. . . Mega-molecules seem to show traces of a long history. How could we possibly imagine them forming suddenly, like the simpler corpuscles, and remaining so once and for all? Their complication and their instability, rather like those of life, both suggest a long process of gradual accretions over a series of generations. . . And so the abyss of the past is deepened by yet another level; and though our incurable intellectual weakness encourages us to compress it into an ever thinner slice of duration, scientific analysis is constantly forcing us to enlarge it.

Pierre Teilhard de Chardin,
The Phenomenon of Man, Collins 1959; Fount 1977,
pp. 88-94

in this atmosphere and collected them in flasks simulating the oceans. The experiment might seem risky: one could predict such different results that the enterprise would be very open to criticism. So Miller performed his experiments secretly. He obtained the spontaneous synthesis of numerous organic bodies, including the amino-acids. In this way he demonstrated that the synthesis of these amino-acids, elementary bricks which go to make up living matter, probably came about through spontaneous chemical reactions in what we conjecture to have been the conditions of primitive earth.

Numerous experiments were made subsequently, at greater or lesser removes from the first model. The natural source of energy posited in Miller's experiment lay in storms. However, other natural sources of energy played a part: volcanoes, radio-active elements and, even more, solar energy, which is received in abundance all over the surface of the earth (ultra-violet and other forms of radiation). These sources of energy have been imitated and the mixtures of gases have been changed: from this scientists have obtained the spontaneous synthesis of almost all the amino-acids, sugars, and adenine. It has been demonstrated that the first two compounds to be formed were cyanhydric acid ($C = NH$) and formaldehyde ($H-CH = O$). Now five molecules of the former make a molecule of adenine (the base of RNA and DNA), and five of the latter make a molecule of ribose (the sugar of RNA) while the two of them together with a molecule of water produce the simplest molecule of amino-acid (glycine).

For hundreds of millions of years, stable organic products, synthesized in this way, must have been accumulating in the oceans.

A *second stage* increased the size of organic molecules. These became larger and more complex through being brought together by certain groups of reactive atoms. The assembling of these dispersed molecules is normally a very slow process, but it could have been accelerated by catalysts like certain surface minerals; this has

been demonstrated by experiments with amino-acids and clay, or again with amino-acids on a piece of lava heated over a period of hours to 170 degrees. This has led to the production of proteinoids, made up of a chain of amino-acids assembled spontaneously.

Similarly, starting from adenine and ribose, with the addition of phosphoric acid and under the action of ultra-violet radiation, scientists have been able to obtain quickly and spontaneously a nucleotide, the elementary link between nucleic acids. Moreover it has proved possible to assemble about ten links of this kind in a short nucleic acid chain, by a spontaneous reaction using a simple chemical agent (cyanamide) and a catalyst formed by a clay surface. Of course this is a long way from the double chain of several million nucleotides arranged in a precise order which form a bacterial chromosome. But we can see that very large molecules could have formed progressively during a long period of biogenesis.

A *third stage* can then begin: the formation of microdrops or coacervates. What happens is that in certain conditions the macromolecules in solution in water come together in agglomerates often a thousand times larger than a macromolecule (agglomerates measuring between 0.5 and 700 microns). This has been demonstrated by experiments with the formation of coacervates (according to Oparin) from biological proteins, and with the production of microspheres (according to Fox) from proteinoids. Thus a sufficient quantity of macromolecules in solution spontaneously leads to the production of innumerable 'microdrops' (according to de Rosnay), the properties of which herald certain properties of living matter. Each coacervate, in its environment, in effect constitutes an individual with a simple structure formed of a membrane separating an inner milieu from the outside environment. Exchanges of substances take place through this membrane: the coacervate 'feeds' by drawing on certain preferred chemical compounds from the world outside.

This way of intensifying reagents facilitates various syntheses in the inner milieu of the coacervate. It is enabled to grow, and then to divide into two or more coacervates. It can also destroy itself, in which case its activity will have enriched the environment with molecules produced by its inner reactions.

The coacervates constitute primitive open systems which can absorb substances rich in energy which they draw from the exterior; they then reject to this exterior molecules which have been formed in the interior. Thus by introducing two suitable catalysts into a coacervate, one can make it synthesize starch from glucose-phosphate drawn from outside, and then degrade this starch to maltose, which is in turn rejected outwards with surplus phosphate. So these open systems are pervaded by a flux of matter and energy. A good deal of research is going on at present into the possibilities of chemical reactions within the coacervates.

A *fourth stage* would have been the improvement of the coacervates, which would have existed in myriads in the primitive oceans. One or other simple and adapted catalyst could have favoured various syntheses in the interior milieu of the coacervates. There would seem to have been an advantage in the more rapid syntheses, which little by little could favour certain more efficient proteins. At the same time, the molecules of nucleotides would tend to assemble in chains. It might be imagined that a system of three macromolecules (for example, two chains of nucleic acids and a protein) would have been formed when these molecules were linked by the reciprocal action of a catalyst: protein would have catalysed the synthesis of a first nucleic chain controlling the rapid synthesis of a second nucleic chain which would determine the rapid synthesis of protein. Billions upon billions of more or less fruitful attempts would have been made in the countless coacervates at the time of biogenesis. The first successes in rapid catalysis would have resulted in the first primitive organisms which scientists call protobiontes, although

they have not discovered any examples.

A *fifth stage* would be the evolution of these protobiontes. They would already have a small genetic programme, with catalyses by simple enzymes. We cannot represent these protobiontes, but we know that they would of necessity have had to feed at the expense of a rich external milieu (heterotrophy). Perhaps they have left behind, down to our day, descendants which still partially resemble them, organisms subsisting on the environment around them but without discovering so rich an environment as that within present living cells. Viruses could possibly be such organisms, the enzymes of which would have been replaced by those of the cells harbouring them (which would be more efficient). However, it is difficult to discover whether the viruses are evidence of earlier organisms or more recent products of a degeneration of parasites.

The significance of the way in which life began for later evolution

The way in which life appeared has important consequences for the subsequent evolution of living beings.

If we accept the old theory of the improbable appearance of a unique first cell in a thin organic soup, we must necessarily derive all living beings from this unique strain. It would probably have been a kind of bacteria and would not necessarily have derived from protobiontes, unless one envisages protobiontes capable of autosynthesis, which would strongly resemble bacteria of the more primitive kind.

This is illustrated by the diagram in Figure 5, which depicts what is known as a monophyletic scheme, so-called because it presents all living beings as having descended from a single original *phylum* or branch. Obviously it has been simplified, and numerous details have been omitted.

If we accept the most recent theory, which argues that in all probability life first appeared in

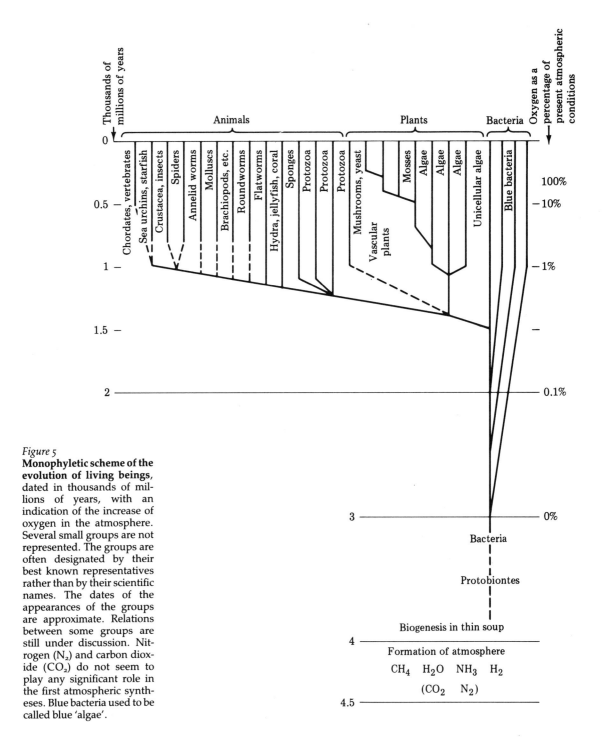

Figure 5
Monophyletic scheme of the evolution of living beings, dated in thousands of millions of years, with an indication of the increase of oxygen in the atmosphere. Several small groups are not represented. The groups are often designated by their best known representatives rather than by their scientific names. The dates of the appearances of the groups are approximate. Relations between some groups are still under discussion. Nitrogen (N_2) and carbon dioxide (CO_2) do not seem to play any significant role in the first atmospheric syntheses. Blue bacteria used to be called blue 'algae'.

a rich organic soup, we are led to imagine it having taken the form of a great many protobiontes which were already differentiated into a variety of types. This then evolved, passing through a bacterial stage, again with numerous different types. Thus the simplest forms of living beings would first appear as stages of evolution. The ancestors of all these organisms would have passed through the same primitive stages, but that does not mean that they would be related. Some groups we can observe now remain evidence of a particular stage of organization, because their evolution specialized and adapted them at this level without allowing them to attain a more complex stage.

This is illustrated by the diagram in Figure 6, which depicts what is known as a polyphyletic scheme, so-called because it presents all living beings as having descended from several different strains subsequent to the stage of bacteria or even protobiontes.

Some questions raised by the origin of life

One of the questions which will automatically occur to anyone reflecting on this appearance of life on earth will be: Did life appear only once on earth?

Many scientists think that the answer to this question is yes, but it is open to a good deal of discussion. In his discussion with the astrophysicist, Herbert Reeves, the sociologist Edgar Morin commented: 'The arguments suggesting that life only appeared once are now stronger than those suggesting that it came into being several times. If life appeared on earth on several occasions, these occasions cannot have amounted to more than two or three. At all events, we cannot rule out the view that the conditions conducive to the emergence of life were removed by the very development of the first strain of life, which would have consumed all organic matter.'

If we accept this view, a new question arises: Why did evolution take this particular course,

passing through protein, DNA, the membrane and increasingly complex structures? The uninitiated are usually staggered by what seems to be the extreme improbability of such a development. 'The theory long defended by the molecular biologists might well seem to be that life arose as a result of a chance as improbable as a monkey at a typewriter writing *Hamlet* without meaning to.'

Now many present-day scientists think that not only is there real continuity, that life is less improbable than it might seem, but that in the end, 'matter was indeed pregnant with life'.

Hubert Reeves supports this approach, and even goes so far as to write: 'It is not absurd to say that the universe has evolved "as if" it wanted to produce a being capable of becoming aware of its own existence' (though he recognizes the utterly anthropomorphic character of this proposition).

For Professor E. Kahane, 'this organization of matter would be the effect of a natural law still to be discovered, by virtue of which the evolution of matter towards increasingly complex forms of movement has necessarily taken this course, because it was the only one possible.'

Someone might then object, 'Why does this "natural law" of organization seem to go against the general tendency of the universe to move towards increasing disorder, in accordance with the second law of thermodynamics?'

One simple answer might be that every increase in order has to be compensated for by greater disorder elsewhere, so that the second law is not violated. That seems to be what happens throughout the universe. Moreover, the second law of thermodynamics relates to closed systems (which do not interact with what is outside them), while living beings and their precursors are open systems (which do interact with what is outside them). So, legitimate though the objection may be, it does not really contradict the view according to which in certain conditions matter would have evolved towards life in accordance with a natural law which we have yet to discover but which we can now begin to guess at.

Figure 6 **Polyphyletic scheme of the evolution of living beings.**

The multiple lines are not necessarily related and appeared at different points on the globe. They will have undergone the various stages of organization independently. Some lines will have preserved the simple organization of their primitive stages, and are the evidence for these. Thus the viruses would seem to be possible evidence of early protoplasm, and the bacteria, by virtue of their structure, evidence of the first living cells. Some of the early cyanobacteria (blue bacteria, formerly called blue 'algae') would have developed into chloroplasts by incorporating themselves in eucaryotic cells which thus became green. The eucaryotes, at first unicellular, originally fell into three categories: green plants (autotrophic), non-green plants (heterotrophic) and animals (heterotrophic). The autotrophs synthesize their living matter themselves. The heterotrophs live on the organic substances produced by the autotrophs or by other heterotrophs. Obviously this scheme must not be pressed too far: the species of a large group (phylum or branch) clearly derived from common ancestors, possibly distant ones. Some large groups are themselves clearly related, like annelid worms and arthropods (crustacea, insects, millipedes, spiders, scorpions and so on). Vascular plants include ferns (pteridophyta) and phanerogamia (gymnosperms and angiosperms) which make up the majority of terrestrial vegetation. All this group could derive from a common strain.

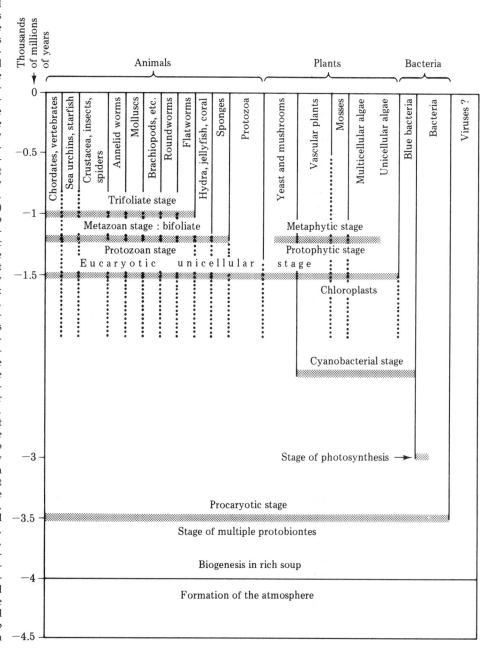

That raises the question whether there is life on other planets with similar characteristics to our own.

At present there is no scientific certainty that life and other civilizations can be found on planets not our own, but this is certainly a possibility.

Hubert Reeves thinks that an argument can be produced in favour of the existence of other civilizations: 'It is based partly on the uniformity of the laws of nature and partly on the uniformity of physical and chemical compounds throughout the observable universe. Tests on this question are increasingly precise and increasingly thorough. The densities of light, of atoms, of interstellar molecules on the one hand, and of stars and galaxies on the other, show that nature is everywhere organized in the same way. There is nothing special here on earth. . . It is reasonable to suppose that even at the most advanced levels of organization (which are beyond our powers of investigation) things still happen in a similar way.'

The beginning of philosophical questioning

Having come this far, we find it natural to ask more questions. 'What is the source of the intellegibility of the universe? How is it that human beings, the most advanced forms of life, can ask questions about the very origin of life? Why do intelligent human beings, endowed with a reflective awareness which allows them to be intellectually detached from the universe in which they are immersed, find that the universe is already intelligible?'

Before humanity comes a history of more than fifteen thousand million years. It has been made without us, but it is 'as if' it had been made for us. We say 'as if' because, for the moment, we cannot justify this intuition.

We note that the laws of the universe which we have slowly discovered by observation and then elaborated by our logic nevertheless have a foundation in a reality which we have not

Is the Ordering of the World a Miracle?

You find it strange that I consider the comprehensibility of the world (to the degree that we may legitimately speak of such comprehensibility) as a *miracle or an eternal mystery*. Well, *a priori* one should expect a chaotic world which cannot in any way be grasped through thought. One could (indeed should) expect the world to seem subject to the laws that we have imposed on it. That would be a kind of order like the alphabetical order of the words of a language. However, the kind of order created, for example, by Newton's theory of gravity is of quite a different kind. Even if the axioms of the theory are posited by a human being, the success of such an enterprise presupposes an order in the objective world of a high degree which one has *a priori* no right to expect. That is the 'miracle' which grows increasingly persuasive with the increasing development of our knowledge.

Albert Einstein, Fragment of a letter to Solovine dated 30 March 1952, in *Lettres à Maurice Solovine*, Paris 1956

created and from which we ourselves have emerged.

This interaction between our minds and a reality which slowly becomes intelligible and predictable is an enigma. Why is it possible, when we could just as well have remained blind in the face of chaos or immersed in a world which was utterly incomprehensible and unpredictable? Thinkers have worked out various epistemological systems in their efforts to reply to this question.

Realist or idealist schools have proposed several possible models of interaction between subject and object, of relationships between the human mind and the reality of things and the world.

The debate is always open, because both poles remain enigmas. Who could exhaust the riches of reality and the world? Who could plumb the depths of the human mind and its subjectivity?

The debate is still topical, even if various attempts have been made to curb it or dismiss it. However, beyond it lies an even more basic question, which has been raised for thousands of years.

Is there a non-human intelligence which might have preceded humanity in the history of the cosmos, which might have left a visible trace in the universe?

Did this intelligence exist? Does it still exist today, in an invisible way? Does it correspond to the notion cherished by human beings since historical times, of a God or gods?

Is not this the intelligence referred to by the saying in the Book of Wisdom, in the biblical tradition?

For from the greatness and beauty of created things comes a corresponding perception of their Creator (Wisdom 13.5).

Do not children who naively ask their parents questions about the origin of the world often have the intuition that everything has been made by the one whom they may learn to call 'Father'?

There are various answers to this basic, metaphysical question.

Some people who accept the intuition of being and metaphysical logic feel it possible to affirm the existence of this transcendent intelligence, distinct from the cosmos, but present in the cosmos.

Many others, moulded by a critical culture which has been our heritage above all over the last two centuries in the West, will remain doubtful: they will fear that such an affirmation is either the projection of our old religious desire to find a first principle or divine intelligence, or a

Is it Impossible to Know God?

What I tell you there can perhaps serve as a reply to your question: 'Is it impossible to know God, or can one know him even without having faith?'

Without swerving from my conscience, and following its testimony, my reply is that I know that 'I believe' in God, but I also know that this 'I believe' is related to a form of knowledge of an intellectual kind. This fact, and the fact that over the course of the centuries so many people with no knowledge of revelation have recognized (and still recognize) that God exists and have had some idea of him, authorizes me to conclude that one can know God by reason alone, though this knowledge is usually inadequate and imprecise.

John Paul II

lack of the courage we need to accept this terrifying solitude of humanity in the universe, though they believe that to be our true nobility.

One of the settings for the debate between believers and atheists is to be found here, on the philosophical side.

We ourselves think that the question whether or not this transcendent intelligence exists must be raised by human reason. The reply to it will depend a good deal on the intellectual and spiritual pilgrimage of the individual.

It is impossible to offer any compelling proof, but we think that an intelligent and reverent reading of the universe and of humanity can be made, and that it allows us to decipher the signs of this intelligent presence.

The origin of life and a view of creation

When we adopt a position within the perspective of faith it is not immaterial whether the origin of life seems to be chance, in conformity with the first theory, or the inevitable result of the laws of physics and chemistry in a terrestrial setting, in conformity with the second theory. That is why we have been led to raise this question at such an early stage.

Many believers had become accustomed to the first theory. Seeing God as the Creator who gave everything existence at every moment, they also regarded this Creator as the master of chance, intervening in a supernatural way, at times of his choosing, to restart, correct, reorientate creation and history when they parted company with his plans. This perspective is still compatible with the emergence of free beings at the heart of creation, but if we push it to extremes, making God no more than a master of chance, we may end up with the image of a capricious God, and ultimately make creation unintelligible and all human action pointless. Such a view would breed a degree of fatalism, not to mention fetishism. It could produce a weak faith which finds itself disorientated when faced with the new discoveries of science. However, these new discoveries could equally serve as a springboard for faith.

In contrast to this belief in a master of chance, the second, determinist theory of the origin of life is sometimes presented as a rational unification of all knowledge, allowing us to bring together in one rational explanation all that exists. It makes the master of chance otiose and supplants all belief in him. We shall not criticize this view of the origin of life here. For the moment, we shall content ourselves with showing briefly how deeply life is illuminated by the vision of Christian faith, a vision which does not contradict any scientific facts.

Believers who adopt the perspective of the second theory will find the action of God on his creation deeper and stronger. He is the source of being, time and history, but does not need to correct the course of the universe en route. His action is manifested through the slow evolution of matter, issuing in life, without being detectable at any particular instant or at a precise phase of the process. The believer perceives the greatness of the creative genius of God better through a creation which bears within itself, from its beginnings, all the riches of its future. In this view the purpose of the universe appears inscribed on all creation, intimately orientated on the emergence of humanity and our encounter with God: 'The universe would appear pregnant with life and the biosphere pregnant with humanity.'

How, it might be asked, does this perspective fit in with the emergence of freedom at the heart of creation? That is a later stage, ending up with the evolution of the living world. As a result of all its riches and wide range of possibilities, the living world displays situations in which the number of possibilities far exceeds the number of courses that can be acted on; that results in large areas of indeterminacy in which several possibilities are offered to choose from. So this unfolding of creation without supernatural intervention fully respects human freedom. Human beings live in a setting that they can trust and understand, in which actions can become meaningful and they can discover a purpose which stimulates them and gives them a reason for living.

However, we shall avoid alienating believers by stressing a particular stage which science has reached. Science is always transitional, always incomplete. Though the unity of the enterprise of God in creation might appear more magnificent within a determinist perspective, the Creator has nevertheless willed to take a risk by producing freedoms which exploit a degree of indeterminacy. God pursues his plan, persevering with the risk that he has willed, not only by remaining faithful in what he creates but also by intervening among free human beings, whom he takes as his conversation partners and to whom he speaks through signs which cannot be reduced to what can be read off creation. God speaks to human beings not only by external voices but also by internal voices.

If we are to explore this enigma of the emergence of freedom better, locating it in history as the divine plan, we shall have to reflect on the genesis of human freedom, retracing the long stages covered by living beings in their progress, through increasing autonomy, towards its achievement.

2

The Emergence of Autonomy among Living Beings, Leading to the Threshold of Freedom

Human beings form an integral part of the biological world. The evidence for this is now quite indisputable. One species among others, *homo sapiens*, i.e. all humanity as it now is, is the culmination of a long period of biological evolution spread over several hundred million years. Human anatomy, human physiology and numerous features of human behaviour have been fashioned over the course of this long history. Scientific information – geology, palaeontology, prehistory, anthropology, genetics, and so on – leads us with increasing certainty to locate humanity on a temporal trajectory.

In the case of man – a term which in this book, as in scientific writing generally, is used to denote human beings of either sex and which in that context for convenience has a masculine possessive pronoun – fixed concepts are a thing of the past. If we are to try to understand man – the 'human phenomenon' – we must necessarily consider him in movement in time. The parameters of this trajectory will be better defined the longer the period of time we take: the course of a millennium tells us almost nothing about human evolution; a million years tells us much more; while a hundred million years allows us to reconstruct a history and to identify its basic tendencies.

We have already looked at one way of envisaging the derivation of the first living beings from inert matter. We shall now take up again the course followed by biological evolution from these first living beings to the appearance of man. In so doing we shall find ourselves arranging events in such a way that they seem to point towards man as their destination. Attributing such a purpose to evolution is clearly open to criticism. Questions can be asked about the existence of 'directions' taken by the evolution of living beings, and there are lively discussions on this subject. Looking back on the past, we can recognize such directions and take them to represent the apparent framework of a history which allows us to watch the emergence of increasingly developed organisms (their growing complexity, 'cerebralization', the progress towards a 'psyche', and so on). The most remarkable and most successful species, which has invaded the whole earth and explores every area of life, is man. That is reason enough for considering humanity (men and women as they are today) as a culminating point and investigating the story of how our success has been achieved.

The original individual

The first living beings were unicellular; they had an individual existence over against their environment, but in part they were barely distinguished from one another. A mother cell divided into two daughter cells without disappearing; in this way it became two cells in perfect continuity with each other.

The individuality of successive generations, parents and children, came about with sexual reproduction. The phenomena of sexuality, involving an exchange of parts of the hereditary programme, can already be found in numerous

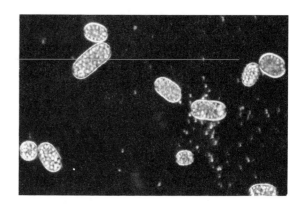

The first living beings were bacteria. This illustration shows sulphur bacteria. *Photo J. -B. Crumeyrolle*

unicellular organisms (even among bacteria), but often they have no more than an auxiliary role, since the succession of generations does not habitually come about through sexuality.

Sexual reproduction preponderates among multicellular beings (and also among certain groups of very specialized unicellular parasites). However, a large number of plants and the most primitive multicellular animals retain broad possibilities of asexual reproduction by the division of an individual into two or more individuals, genetically identical with the first; this assures a certain degree of perpetuity to individuals, while at the same time providing an opportunity for the innovations of sexual reproduction.

In sexual reproduction the individual offspring are, of course, new creatures made up of elements provided by two different individual parents. That speeds up evolution by allowing advantageous mutations to spread in a population through the interplay of cross-breeding.

40

Death and evolution

Multicellular animals experience a growth in their potentialities: their organism becomes structured, their cells specialize and form organs for nutrition, respiration, circulation within the organism, the elimination of waste products, the support of the body, movement, and finally organs which control the body. All this increases the capacities of the animal, but the price of the necessary specialization of cells is a loss of potentialities. Only some of these cells retain the capacity to transmit all the potentialities of the individual without themselves becoming specialized: these are the reproductive cells. By contrast, the other cells are doomed to a more or less rapid death; some are still capable of multiplying to renew a tissue or an organ. The cell with the greatest degree of specialization, the nerve-cell which controls the organism, ends up with the weakest capacity for regeneration. Not only do these cells lose their power to multiply; they use themselves up in their specialized function. This happens to such a degree that all animals, after having attained a certain level of evolution, inexorably die through irreversible wear and tear on one or other of their organs (often the nervous system). It is no longer an individual cell which perpetuates itself, but only the species, through a succession of individuals.

This results in the process of birth, development and death, which affects almost all multicellular beings (and some unicellular beings). So this succession of generations is the rule which forces itself on them. It goes on to play a part in accelerating evolution, imposing on each successive generation a mixture of hereditary characteristics and propagating new characteristics 'invented' by the mutations.

Thus death appears as the generator of biological progress by allowing new beings to succeed parents from which they are slightly different. As a result of the increasing complexity of the body, death is the price paid for the existence of highly organized and autonomous individuals. Here it appears as an indispensable condition for progress towards autonomy.

The transition to the multicellular stage produces a sequence of generations which are born and die. This is the first division of the egg of the sea urchin.
Photo J. -B. Crumeyrolle

Progress towards autonomy. The first vertebrates

Multicellular animals, provided with a nervous system and reproducing themselves sexually, were already widespread in the oceans more than seven hundred million years ago (scientists represent this as 700 Ma). Without doubt they came into being even earlier, perhaps going back more than a thousand million years. Almost all the large groups of animals (annelid worms, molluscs, arthropods, etc.) were represented at the beginning of the primary period (about 530 Ma). However, the group of vertebrates had yet to come into being. This was the group whose evolution was to undergo the most complex developments, tending towards the acquisition of an increasing independence from the surrounding environment. Palaeontology allows us to retrace the main stages of this 'march' towards independence, the chronology of which is fixed for us by geology.

The first remains of vertebrates that we know of are about 480 million years old. The vertebrates in question were 'fishes' of a very special kind, with no jaws and with articulated limbs, known as 'armoured fishes'. Their body was enclosed in a bony carapace from which only a mobile tail protruded, moving with a sculling motion. These animals led a passive life. What they could do in their environment was extremely limited (they could only move and feed). While they were doubtless adapted to very specific conditions of life, they had only a very slender evolutionary potential and soon disappeared.

About 400 million years ago, other 'fishes' appeared, equipped for the first time with jaws and fins (e.g. placoderms). As often in the history of life, we find several rival kinds of 'jaws' and 'fins' simultaneously before the types of organization that we know among present-day fish become established. Very soon, the fins of certain fish become longer and change, prefiguring an elementary limb. One representative of these fish, called 'crossopterygii', is the coelacanth, one of the distant descendants of this group of animals from the heart of which other branches lead to all the walking vertebrates (known as 'tetrapods').

Pierre-Louis Moreau de Maupertuis

This Breton gentleman was born at Saint-Malo in 1698. He was the first to formulate transformist ideas clearly, which he did in a number of works: *Physical Venus* (1746), *Essay on Cosmology* (1750), *System of Nature. Essay on the Formation of Organized Beings* (1751). However, he was especially active as a mathematician. The *System of Nature* was written in Latin under the pseudonym of Baumann and published in Germany. One notable passage is this:

'XLV. Could this not be an explanation of how the multiplication of the most dissimilar species could follow from two single individuals? They would simply have owed their first origin to chance productions in which the elementary parts did not retain the order which they had in the father and mother animals: each degree of error would have made a new species: and the effect of repeated deviations would have given rise to the infinite diversity of animals that we see today. Perhaps this would increase with time, but it might be that subsequent centuries would bring only intangible increases.'

Maupertuis was challenged by Voltaire, who ridiculed him under the name of Doctor Akakia (1751); both were rivals at the court of Frederick II of Prussia, who made Maupertuis Director of the Berlin Academy in 1746. George Buffon, the pioneering French naturalist, praised Maupertuis, but for all that did not argue for a real transformism. Maupertuis died in 1759.

Extract from P. Ostoya, *Les Theories de l'Evolution*, Paris 1951

Emergence from the water and the conquest of dry land

The first land vertebrates were the amphibians (also called batrachians), so called because they divided their life between two environments, water and dry land, though some of them spent all their lives in the water. The first of these amphibians appeared about 375 million years ago; their organization did not differ much from that of the crossopterygii mentioned earlier. Lungs must have appeared in some of these fish who lived in seas which periodically dried up. Limbs were still archaic, but from this point on the affinity with our 'hand' is evident (it was already adumbrated in some crossopterygii). The persistence of the caudal fin is the sign of a habitat which is still largely aquatic.

This first 'landing' on dry ground had long been prepared for in the water (the formation of limbs and lungs). However, it was still necessary to be able to survive on dry land! The air there could be breathed, since now there began to be enough oxygen. Without question, the problem of food was more acute, since these first amphibians were carnivorous. They could still find food in the water, but they could only really leave the water provided that they could find food on earth. Only millions of years later did the first definitely terrestrial animals, the arthropods (more specifically insects), appear. They were only able to establish themselves on land after the development of vegetation capable of feeding them. A whole ecological system had to be set up on dry ground before the tetrapod vertebrates could live there: first of all came the first vegetation on dry land (about 410 million years ago), and then came the insects which fed on this vegetation (about 380 to 350 Ma). Finally the amphibians appeared (they emerged progressively between about 375 Ma and 350 Ma). It is very probable that before becoming land animals from then on, these amphibians had to wait until the insect population became numerous enough to feed them. All this had come about by the carboniferous age (about 350 Ma).

Having reached the walking stage, the vertebrates were already partially liberated from an aquatic environment. However, they still remained partially bound to it for reproduction and the larval stage (like the present-day frog). New problems arose, for example that of the suspension of the skull on the vertebral column. The weight of the voluminous skull was partially supported by the shoulders, but this very much limited the mobility of the animal. The 'remodelling' of the skeleton inherited from the crossopterygii – fish for which the mechanical problem of the suspension of the skull clearly did not arise – was far from being achieved.

About 300 million years ago, a new type of organization developed: the reptile of the carboniferous period. The essential modifications related to movement and reproduction:

– The rearrangement of limbs, the disengagement of the neck, freeing the head from the shoulders, which became more mobile. The skull was suspended only from the vertebral column, which became the mainstay of the skeleton.

– The appearance of the reptilian egg (the 'amnion'). This is really the first successful experiment in complete autonomy from the aquatic milieu (by providing protection through the shell, an internal liquid milieu, and autonomous reserves for nutrition).

All these innovations moved in the direction of a much greater mobility (in movement generally, and in getting food) and final liberation from an aquatic environment. The reptile is no longer bound, like the amphibian, to its watery sea (reptiles live in the Sahara). The development of pulmonary respiration (instead of breathing more widely through the skin, like amphibians) and the protection for the skin provided by scales further consolidated liberation from an aquatic milieu.

Thermal independence. The mammals

About 260 million years ago, in the Permian period, we have the first sketchy outlines of

43

Jean-Baptiste de Monet, Chevalier de Lamarck

Photo Roger-Viollet

He was born in 1744 at Bazentin in Picardy. First a botanist, in 1778 he published a *Flora of France*. The work pleased Buffon, who made Lamarck a member of the Academy of Sciences in 1781. At this time Lamarck was opposed to spontaneous generation and favoured the idea of the constancy and hence the fixity of species. He published a *Botanical Encyclopaedia* from 1783 on. He was nominated to the chair of 'Lower Animals' (insects and worms) at the Museum; he began to study and classify these animals, introducing the distinction between vertebrates and invertebrates.

His essential ideas from 1800 on are formulated in the Opening Lectures of his courses at the Museum. He defined them more clearly and developed them in the lectures which followed, in his better known *Zoological Philosophy* (1809) and in his *Natural History of Animals without Vertebrae* (1815-1822).

Lamarck was very struck by the difficulty of making neat distinctions between species, and also by the variations between them. He saw among living beings a 'subtle gradation of complexity' and an internal tendency to become more complex. He thought in terms of a transformation of species, partly under the influence of the environment (which could modify the organism directly) and partly by the efforts of animals. He put particular stress on this second aspect. Need created an organ and use developed it. Failure to use an organ resulted in its disappearance. This active adaptation to the environment is illustrated by the giraffe, with its long neck, and the mole, which is almost blind. Modifications thus achieved progressively were transmitted to descendants. These ideas seem to have been quite widespread in popular French culture, though scientifically they had no basis in experiments. Lamarck was vigorously challenged by his distinguished contemporary Georges Cuvier, who mocked him over the giraffe which 'stretched its neck'.

Lamarck argued for spontaneous generation, but only at the level of the simplest living beings. Certainly the most simple beings then known were already very complex. His ideas were partly to be taken up by Darwin, but Darwin made selection the external guide to the transformation of species, while Lamarck gave it an internal guide, active adaptation by effort.

In 1829 Lamarck died poor, blind and three times widowed, but devotedly cared for by his daughter and admired by pupils like Geoffroy-Saint-Hilaire.

---

organization of a mammalian kind in a group of vertebrates who have been called 'mammal-like reptiles'. This time the progress in the direction of autonomy was decisive.

Homeothermy (a process keeping the temperature of the body constant at between 35 and 40 degrees centigrade) ensured a definitive freedom *vis à vis* the external temperature. On the one hand this allowed the animal to maintain its activity independently of external cold (when it is cold, reptiles cannot be active). On the other hand, it allowed it to adapt to a great diversity of climate (there are mammals in Greenland and in the Sahara). Birds achieved homeothermy independently through another line of reptiles;

moreover, several 'systems' of homeothermy were achieved or roughed out among the reptiles before the types found in mammals and birds prevailed.

The rearrangement of limbs, the mobility of the head, the differentiation of teeth into incisors, canines and molars, the reorganization of the ear and the jaw, ensured superior efficiency in movement, getting food, and defence.

The progressive appearance of placentary viviparity and suckling (typical of the mammal) ensured more effective reproduction, completely independent of the external environment. On the other hand, suckling, which presupposes a prolonged contact with the mother, also plays an important role in the acquisition of behaviour by the young (learning and socialization). Archaic mammals which have survived to the present day (like duck-billed platypuses and kangaroos) give some idea of the progressive appearance of these mammalian characteristics.

Despite all these advantages, the mammal took a long time to establish itself. Mammal-like reptiles, which flourished and diversified in the Permian period, sometimes attaining the size of a bear, disappeared after the Triassic period, for reasons which are hard to discover, but are probably connected with the climate.

Between about 200 and 70 million years ago the world of mammals, which by now was clearly distinguished, was represented only by very small creatures. These did not compete with the reptiles, who at that time occupied almost all the 'ecological niches' of the great vertebrates on land. Climatic conditions, which were tropical, probably did not allow the 'innovations' which had developed in mammals to prove their efficiency. This was the 'age of the reptiles'. The mammals were to take their vengeance in a spectacular way when the climate deteriorated, becoming colder again towards the end of the secondary era.

From the dawn of the Tertiary period (about 60 Ma), the small mammals, with the large reptiles now out of their way, began to occupy the land. They diversified extremely rapidly into a multitude of forms, of all sizes, and these occupied all the ecological niches (there were herbivores, carnivores, insectivores, flying mammals, swimmers, underground mammals, etc.). We should note that all these 'evolutionary lines' amounted to so many irreversible commitments, leading to increasing specialization in an increasingly narrow area (cf. horses, dolphins, elephants and so on).

The group of primates partly kept aloof from this general tendency. On the whole their organization remained relatively unspecialized, sometimes primitive (skull, teeth, limbs), and they retained a much wider range of options.

Primates from the first part of the Tertiary period have attracted the attention of palaeontologists much less than other mammals; their history is less well known.

Standing upright, increase in brain size, use of artefacts

Between about 10 Ma and 3 Ma a particular group of primates (with relatively unspecialized limbs and teeth) began to undergo transformations which, *mutatis mutandis*, recall those of the 'reptilian revolution'. The starting point for this momentous transformation seems to have been the acquisition of a way of moving vertically on the rear limbs, in what is called the upright position. That might appear trivial, since this form of movement had already been used, with very different means, by other groups of vertebrates (dinosaurs, birds and so on), without leading to any modification of the way in which the skull was suspended. This time, however, it was the beginning of a chain reaction the last link in which was to be man:

1. The front limbs, which no longer had to support the body, became solely prehensile, a role which had formerly devolved on the mouth. The hand became specialized enough to be a precision instrument with a sense of touch controlled by the nervous system, but at the same time it could still be used for a variety of functions: it made use of artificial extensions for almost infinite uses, in the form of artefacts.

2. The suspension of the skull was rearranged: the head was no longer suspended in front of the vertebral column but balanced on it; this called for less powerful muscles by which to attach it. From that point on the mechanical obstacles in the way of the expansion of the brain pan could be surmounted.

3. At the nape of the neck, the modification of the way in which the skull was suspended much reduced the mass of muscles needed to hold the head up, and this freed and lightened the bones

Charles Robert Darwin

Photo Roger-Viollet

He was born at Shrewsbury in 1809, the year of the publication of Lamarck's *Zoological Philosophy*. An undistinguished candidate for holy orders without a strong vocation, but already attracted by the natural sciences, at the age of twenty-two, in December 1831, Charles Darwin sailed as a 'naturalist' on board HMS *Beagle*. The voyage lasted five years and took him to South America and the islands of the Pacific and Indian Oceans. It decided his destiny. The notoriety of Charles Darwin tends to overshadow the reputation of his grandfather, the doctor and naturalist Erasmus Darwin (1731-1802), who was a precursor to Lamarck.

Returning to Great Britain with incomparable experience as a naturalist, Darwin spent his life constructing a coherent theory of the origin and transformations of living species. At that time, in the first half of the nineteenth century, there was a bitter dispute on the subject. The idea of evolution was already widespread, thanks in particular to the work of Lamarck and others. However, the 'official theory' was still that of creationism and fixed species, of the kind defended, for example, by Cuvier. The progress of geology, palaeontology and comparative anatomy or embryology had already led to the emergence of the idea of a progression of living forms over geological time. However, many people, including those with most influence, refused to accept that these different forms could be connected in a genealogy, or to envisage a connection between them by filiation over the course of a geological history the real duration of which was unknown. Hence the idea that there were successive creations leading to the appearance of the new species. The French palaeontologist Alcide d'Orbigny enumerated twenty-seven of these. The absence of intermediary forms, of any recognition of features common to the different kinds of fossils, strengthened this view, which was still in agreement with what was said in the Bible.

Only in 1859, twenty-three years after the return of *The Beagle*, did Charles Darwin make known his theory of 'the origin of species by means of natural selection or the preservation of races favoured in the struggle for life'. It can be summed up in several simple principles. Within a population representing a given living species, one can see individual variations, usually minimal, which appear by chance. Breeders and horticulturalists know this, and seek to profit from it by selecting new products with an apparently new character which they believe to be advantageous. Nature exercises a similar selection 'on a grand scale'. In fact conditions of life in the natural environment (space, food, sexual attraction, etc.) produce rivalry between individuals, a 'struggle for life', from which the fittest, those with some advantage, benefit. They have the most numerous descendants and progressively establish a population with their characteristics. The origin and evolution of species can be understood in this way, by filiation, without recourse to successive creations.

This theory immediately provoked enthusiasm and polemic in scientific, philosophical and religious circles. Its impression of coherence in fact concealed a great weakness: Darwin was unable to give a satisfactory explanation of the transmission of characteristics. There was as yet no theory of heredity. During successive editions of his work, Darwin tried, unsuccessfully, to make up for this deficiency. However, from 1865 on, the Austrian monk Mendel opened the way to genetic theories, though his views were unknown to Darwin. The scientific world only rediscovered them in 1900, eighteen years after Darwin's death.

That did not prevent Darwin's work from exercising a decisive influence on the evolution of ideas. When he died in 1882, covered with honours, the transformists, supporters of evolution, had triumphed over the creationists, at least in the scientific world. The debate was then to shift to the sphere of the mechanisms of evolution. It is still by no means closed.

which supported these muscles, allowing them to take another form.

4. At the front of the head, since the hand now served for prehensile purposes and artefacts were used for defence and manufacture of objects, the mouth and the teeth regressed, leaving room for frontal development.

5. At the temples, since artefacts made it possible to reduce the work of the jaws, the masticating muscles slackened and found a place lower on the skull, leaving room for the enlargement of the brain pan.

And that is how, on all sides, it was possible for the brain to grow larger.

These essential transformations took place three or four million years ago (or perhaps a little earlier) in the group called Australopitheci. After this, right down to present-day man, the anatomy of the skeleton only underwent minor adjustments. The evolutionary phenomenon which is called 'hominization' took advantage of the possibilities offered at the Australopithecus stage, i.e. above all the possibilities of developing the brain pan. This was a necessary condition for the growth and increasing complexity of the brain ('encephalization'). At the level of scientific analysis, this is another story, the interpretation of evidence of mental activity (artefacts, rites, art) firmly based on the observation of anatomical structures.

Figure 7 retraces, backwards towards the beginning, the evolutionary route that we have just followed from the origin of the earth to the Australopitheci.

To sum up, 480 million years of the history of the vertebrate world displays, through countless ups and downs, a constant and coherent tendency towards an increasing autonomy displayed by the organism in relation to the outside world. That is translated into increasingly complex activities in the sphere of relational functions (movement and perception) and reproduction. The increase in these activities, producing combinations of increasing complexity, was possible only as a result of a parallel development of the brain throughout the history of the vertebrates in general and the human branch in particular. The exceptional success of the human form must have come about as a result of the centralization of information and of control of the individual, i.e. the development of an important brain: a centralization of this kind is usually to be found among the most evolved species of each large group of animals.

Freedom has been achieved:

1. From the liquid milieu from which life came. Initially bound to the aquatic milieu, the vertebrate then integrated it into its organism: it was no longer *in the water* but carried the water *in its body* (circulation of blood, ova, etc.), along with the means of conserving it;

2. From climatic conditions. Homeothermy meant that activity was no longer regulated by the temperature of the environment; viviparity meant that it was no longer the sun which ensured a more or less regular and random incubation;

3. Finally, from its own anatomy. The artefact is an anatomical extension of the hand, with many uses. It supplements at will all the specializations of the body (it can serve as a tusk, a claw, a hook, and so on); projectiles can abolish some spatial limitations, and so on.

Having arrived at the stage of the Australopitheci, the vertebrate had developed to the full the process of independence from its environment. The essentials of the anatomical (corporeal) adventure had been achieved. The last two or three million years have been devoted to developing its consequences by an evolution of another kind, more difficult to grasp, which is that of the genesis of reflective awareness.

Theories about the Mechanism of Evolution: Neo-Lamarckianism, Neo-Darwinism, Neutralism

Lamarck's ideas, like those of Darwin, led to subsequent versions which enjoyed varying success.

Towards the end of the nineteenth century, a neo-Lamarckian school attracted a large number of supporters of transformism, especially palaeontologists. This school thought that the motive force behind evolution did not lie in natural selection but in the aptitude of individuals to accommodate themselves progressively to their environment by morphological and physiological adaptations. The modifications acquired were transmitted to their descendants. Darwin himself had accepted the part played by the environment in the transformation of organisms. The reconstruction of the phyla of fossil species, displaying a progressive and coherent modification in a given direction, pointed more towards a gradual adaptation to the environment than towards an intervention of fortuitous variations under the control of natural selection.

The works of August Weismann, also at the end of the nineteenth century, showed that only sexual cells transmitted hereditary characteristics, independently of the rest of the organism. It became impossible to see how characteristics acquired under the influence of the environment or by active adaptation to it could be inherited, since because these characteristics were not part of the legacy of heredity, they could not be transmitted. So in its most elementary form, the neo-Lamarckian position became untenable.

The neo-Darwinian school came into being at the beginning of the twentieth century, as a result of a combination of Darwin's ideas with genetics, or the science of heredity. Rejecting the possibility of inheriting acquired characteristics and modifications produced by the environment, neo-Darwinism incorporated ideas of the mutations of genes and chromosomes, the laws of simple genetics, quantitative genetics, the genetics of populations, and the flourishing fields of cellular and molecular genetics. This transformed it to such a degree that even the absence of

selection was incorporated into the theory. The term 'synthetic theory' was therefore often preferred as a designation of this group.

According to this synthetic theory, evolution is set in motion by a motive force which forms the totality of mutations (no matter whether these come about through the change of a gene or through a rearrangement of chromosomes). This motive force does not give any direction, since these mutations are produced by chance. The direction of evolution is ensured by a 'rudder', external to the organisms, provided by the natural selection exercised by the conditions of the environment. In certain cases, however, this selection does not act; for example, because there is no rivalry between an excessively small number of individuals in an environment which is vast and under-populated (only the unfit are eliminated). In the absence of a rudder, then, evolution progresses by chance: the term used is genetic 'derivation' or neo-Darwinian evolution, if the term neo-Darwinism is limited to situations in which there is some selection.

Cellular genetics comes to the support of this conception, by demonstrating how living beings are built up in accordance with a programme locked up in chromosomes (DNA, see Ch. 1), this programme being set in motion by messages (messenger RNA) which go from the chromosomes to the 'assembly lines' of proteins (cf. Fig. 3). The 'basic dogma' of cellular genetics states that the information can go only in one direction, from the DNA to the RNA and then to the protein (and never in the opposite direction): here a DNA gene corresponds exactly with a protein. The complexity of living beings has already partially challenged this dogma, since certain information (the virus) passes from the RNA to the DNA and certain genes (again the virus) can function in two different ways, producing two different proteins.

A modern neo-Lamarckism is based essentially on a criticism of neo-Darwinism and its failings, seeking to re-establish the idea of an active adaptation or an action

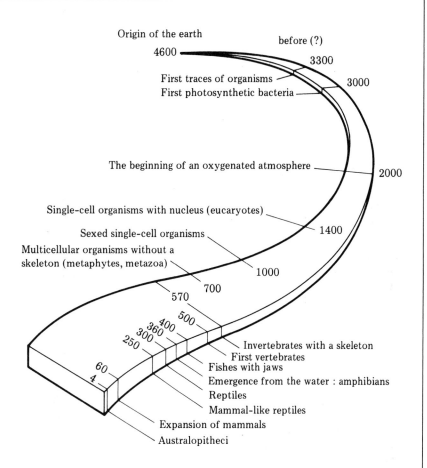

Figure 7 **The main landmarks in biological evolution**
The figures indicate approximate ages in millions of years; future discoveries could produce even earlier fossils.

Origin of the earth
4600

before (?)
3300

First traces of organisms
First photosynthetic bacteria

3000

2000

The beginning of an oxygenated atmosphere

1400

Single-cell organisms with nucleus (eucaryotes)

Sexed single-cell organisms

Multicellular organisms without a skeleton (metaphytes, metazoa)

1000

700

570

500
400
360
300
250

Invertebrates with a skeleton
First vertebrates
Fishes with jaws
Emergence from the water : amphibians
Reptiles
Mammal-like reptiles

60
4

Expansion of mammals
Australopitheci

which the environment forces on hereditary characteristics. For example it can twist the fundamental dogma, envisaging patterns of genetic modification as a result of the action of the environment on the DNA, or by the retroaction of the protein on the DNA. Scientists are certainly aware of ways of modifying DNA by radiation or chemicals, but the results obtained always betray the effect of adaptation, directed in a particular way; the only result is an increase in the number of mutations, rather than an orientation.

It is possible that the random mutations may be less random than we imagine, that in part they are an indication of our ignorance of many mechanisms. It is possible that the laws of physics and chemistry represent, if not an internal guide, at least a more restricted guide than we suppose to the possibility of mutations. In fact we know of types of mutations which are more frequent than others in certain spheres, while many chromosomes contain some areas with numerous mutations and others with none at all.

A recent theory, the so-called 'neutralist' theory, put forward by a mathematician who calculates theoretical models (Kimura), argues that non-Darwinian mutation, i.e. mutation without selection, is general in the majority of genes. If it is true that some genes escape selection, many others are clearly subject to it.

3

The Evolution of Behaviour and Freedom

Biological evolution shows us a progression of living beings in the animal kingdom towards an increasing freedom over against the environment which gives them life. This autonomy of living beings makes possible the existence of types of behaviour and is based on the types of behaviour which it needs. Thus the type of behaviour is the expression of the autonomy of a living organism. So we need to make a comparative study of behaviour, specifying its evolution through the various groups of animals, if we are to be able to follow the progress in independence among these beings, not only from the environment in which they live, but also from against the specific factors which determine them.

The simplest organisms display very elementary forms of behaviour. These are either tropisms, i.e. automatic attraction or rejection by a particular substance or phenomenon, or simple reflex actions, i.e. immediate reactions to stimulation. The protozoa and numerous invertebrates remain at this level, though they also have some elements of memory, based on chemical substances.

Innate behaviour

The complexity of the way in which many animal species exist calls for equally complex behaviour. This is needed either to maintain primogeniture, or simply to ensure the continued existence of the individual. Thus the behaviour of a large number of invertebrate species is adapted to their mode of existence. This behaviour manifests itself directly after the birth or hatching of the individual, and is the result of the implementation of a genetic programme which adapts it well to the normal conditions of the environment, without much room for variation. Such behaviour has been called innate or instinctive (in the scientific sense). Thus the butterfly 'knows' how to fly as soon as its wings have become rigid after its emergence from its chrysalis. Similarly, the wasp which catches caterpillars is attracted by these caterpillars, 'knows' how to catch them and sting them effectively, and to dig the holes where it buries its victims on which it lays its eggs. All this takes place in a precise

Instinct and Innate Behaviour

Reasoning and a conscious sense of purpose have often been attributed to the instinctive behaviour of animals, and particularly insects. This error is called 'anthropomorphism'. Despite often anthropomorphic language, however, early writers were aware of the limits of instinct, as is shown by this extract from Latreille. In the language of his time, he expresses what a modern scientist (Grassé, see below) defines with more precision.

In 1817, in his *New and General Considerations on Insects living in Society*, André Latreille wrote:

'Although the labour of insects might seem to indicate an industry of which the animals of the higher classes offer us few examples, I am a long way from comparing them to the latter, in terms of using the faculties of the intellect, and from attributing to them those combinations of ideas and judgments that a much more developed and complicated organism allows other animals. At birth insects have all the knowledge that their destiny requires; this consists in a certain number of ideas relative to their needs and the use of their organs. The range of their actions is determined: they cannot go beyond it. This natural disposition which enables them to execute in a particular and constant manner what is necessary to support their life and propagate their race is what I call instinct. They cannot have a better guide. Being far too much passengers on the scene of nature, they would have no time either to deliberate on or to profit from the lessons of experience; any wrong calculation would compromise the fate of their posterity.'

Pierre P. Grassé gives us the present scientific understanding of instinct.

'Instinct is now defined as an innate and specific form of behaviour, performed to perfection without previous learning. Its normal realization depends on conditions in the outside world and the physiological state of the executant.'

The silkworm 'weaves a cocoon, to perfection, without any preliminary trials. The young spider, Epeira, weaves a web without having seen its mother do the same thing. The sphex, the wasp which captures insects on which it lays its eggs, chases and paralyses grasshoppers without any previous experience. The pike captures its prey without its parents having taught it how. . .'

These specific phenomena prove not only the innate quality but also the 'constitutional' and hereditary character of instinct.

Instinct is an integral part of the patrimony of the species; 'it is written in the genes like all the other hereditary characteristics. . .'

'In instinctual behaviour, each act has its own immediate determinism; the executant does not have any awareness of the result of its actions; only the pattern of actions making up a complex would seem to be "finalized".'

Pierre P. Grassé, *Encyclopedie de la Pleiade, Zoologie*, I, 1963, 249f., 274f., 282f.

order, as a series of automatic actions, never learned but nevertheless well regulated. Similarly, the reproduction of many invertebrates – and even vertebrates – takes place in accordance with a certain ritual, characteristic of the species. This often calls for quite specific conditions, so that the sexual partners can exchange successive signals leading them to fertilization. These signals and this ritual are not learned, not least because often they are only used once: they are regulated in advance for each individual. Such predetermined behaviour clearly leaves no room for individual initiative: the individual functions as a cog in its species, the existence and reproduction of which it ensures.

Acquired behaviour

However, that does not represent the totality of behaviour, even among the invertebrates. In fact, by creating experimental situations, scientists have noted that some insects are capable not only of adapting their behaviour to these situations but also of registering the new state of things and partly governing their behaviour by what they have registered. Thus bees are capable of rediscovering the entrance to their hive after an orientation flight which they make when they first go out. Moreover, they can be made to recognize a geometrical figure marking the entrance to their hive; this sign helps them to return home. They can also be trained to gather honey at fixed points and at certain precise times. All these features represent what has been called acquired behaviour. One of the simplest instances of this can be found in the conditioned reflexes of dogs who react to a bell as though they had seen food, once the bell and the food have been associated for them over a period of time. Numerous forms of training (animal dressage, etc.) are connected with acquired behaviour. These correspond to a considerable increase in the capabilities of the individual which acquires them. Acquired behaviour can only exist in the right conditions for it to be acquired; thus it is not an inevitable consequence of the genetic struc-

ture of the individual, but is established, rather, through a process of acquisition. However, acquired behaviour is not totally independent of genetic characteristics, since these characteristics restrict the range of possibilities of acquiring it.

So it may be said that innate behaviour corresponds to a 'programme' the realization of which is rigid and allows of only a few variations, while acquired behaviour corresponds to 'authorizations of programmes' which are most extended, and which are conditioned by circumstances and by the factors involved in their acquisition. The behaviour of more than one species has evolved along with an increase in the range of possibilities for acquired behaviour; this range has come far to exceed what can effectively be realized in time. That leads to a much greater possibility of autonomy, not only over against the environment, but also over against the genetic determination of innate behaviour. If we compare the different groups of vertebrates, we can note a considerable development in the presence of acquired behaviour between the least evolved (fish and amphibians) and the most evolved (mammals). This takes place at the expense of innate behaviour (it does not stand in the way of the existence of complex acquisition in the case of primitive species). The phenomenon increases among the superior primates, attaining its culminating point with man: almost all human behaviour in fact seems to have been developed slowly from a starting point (birth) where it was not evident at all.

That would suggest that human behaviour is largely independent of genetic determination. However, here we arrive at a problem in interpreting innate and acquired behaviour which has raised passionate discussions. Although these aim at being scientific, they are in fact subject to ideological influences. For example it can be said that a particular form of behaviour which is thought to be acquired because it developed at a late stage is much less acquired than is supposed: it could not manifest itself earlier because it lacked the means; when these means appeared, the behaviour could be estab-

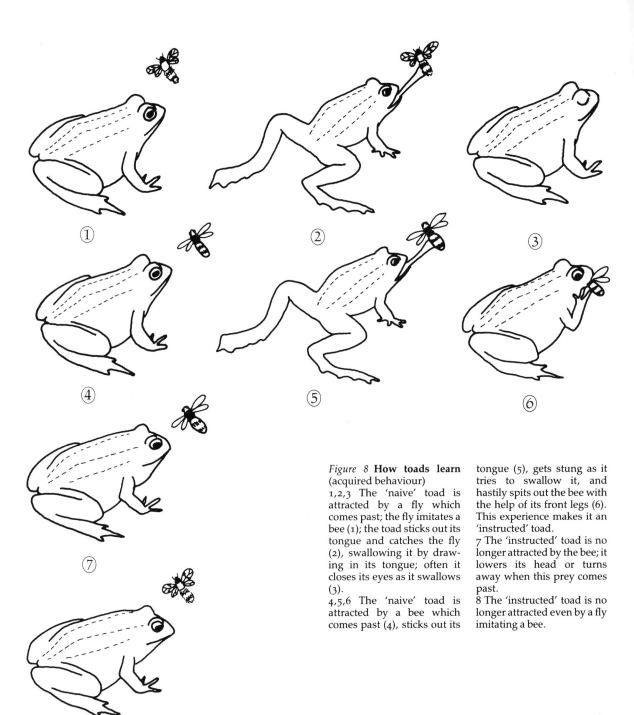

Figure 8 **How toads learn** (acquired behaviour)

1,2,3 The 'naive' toad is attracted by a fly which comes past; the fly imitates a bee (1); the toad sticks out its tongue and catches the fly (2), swallowing it by drawing in its tongue; often it closes its eyes as it swallows (3).

4,5,6 The 'naive' toad is attracted by a bee which comes past (4), sticks out its tongue (5), gets stung as it tries to swallow it, and hastily spits out the bee with the help of its front legs (6). This experience makes it an 'instructed' toad.

7 The 'instructed' toad is no longer attracted by the bee; it lowers its head or turns away when this prey comes past.

8 The 'instructed' toad is no longer attracted even by a fly imitating a bee.

54

lished, as if it were innate. Conversely, it can be questioned whether a form of behaviour which is apparently innate is in fact so, by indicating influences which the embryo could have undergone unconsciously in the course of its development. Added to this difficulty in distinguishing between innate and acquired behaviour is the fact that in numerous circumstances innate and acquired behaviour are intimately interwoven. This has led ethologists (specialists in behaviour) to consider 'innate' and 'acquired' as notions which are too abstract and which do not provide an adequate description of actual behaviour. Finally, it must not be imagined that acquired behaviour is always flexible while innate behaviour is always rigid, since what is acquired can prove to be just as automatic as what is innate, and be just as much a limiting factor on autonomy.

The cultural element

While they have not entirely discarded these concepts of innate and acquired behaviour, which have helped them to make great progress and still have some meaning, many ethologists are now particularly interested in discovering how natural behaviour became established. Here they have come to distinguish between what is received through the genes by heredity, what is fashioned by external influences and not received from others of the species (nor transmitted to others), and finally what is transmitted by the influence – or communication – of others of the species (parents or other models) as the result of a 'cultural' process. This cultural element is a way of transmitting certain forms of behaviour independently of the genetic process, though the genetic constitution of individuals is a contributory factor. It is recognized that this constitution makes possible a vast range of behaviour which can be acquired and transmitted by means of culture; the range usually exceeds what can be realized at any one time and often even what has so far been explored. It is

because of the extreme openness of these possibilities that favoured attitudes can be 'handed on' culturally from generation to generation.

If the cultural element is to be defined properly, it must be distinguished, for example, from patterns of learning which can be imposed on animals without their being able to transmit what they have learned to another individual. These forms of learning represent acquisitions restricted to particular individuals which are incapable of being handed down. Culture is more than that. While it is as optional as a learning process (it has to be), it can be transmitted to another individual; thus it is the transmission of acquired behaviour, usually in the form of learning by imitation, which is a much more economical process than learning by trial and error (or by punishment). That demonstrates the need for models throughout the cultural development of a form of behaviour. On the other hand, if it is to prove possible to imitate these models they need to contain a minimum of purposive behaviour, orientated either simply on the model as it is, or on the advantage that it provides.

The development of the cultural aspect becomes very striking when we pass from the 'middle' vertebrates (reptiles and birds) to the superior vertebrates (mammals) and particularly to the superior primates and to man. Birds display numerous forms of stereotyped behaviour, in which certain patterns of acquired behaviour can cloak the characteristics of rigorous constraint. Thus ducks (for example the sheldrake) need to learn to recognize others of their family from a very early age; if they make a mistake here (for example sheldrakes identifying with mallards), they are no longer able to identify a suitable sexual partner and therefore have no offspring. The songs of some birds are evidently determined genetically, in such a way that the species cannot sing otherwise. There are also birds which learn their parents' song, this being the only way in which the song can be handed down; finally, certain birds are capable of learning very different songs, or even music.

The way in which behaviour emerges as a result of culture is more evident among mammals. All species of mammals have a family life for a certain period, and many of them are social. Among mammals the generations depend on one another and those of the same species need to undergo a process of learning, always in interaction with the environment and the problems that it raises. Those of the species who transmit the cultural element are at least the parents, but often also all those who make up the social environment. More forms of behaviour are involved, the more evolved the species is. We know of the faculty possessed by numerous so-called 'vermin' to avoid poisoned bait once they have been shown its effects: not only an individual but a whole local population is 'taught' the danger of the bait, so that it becomes ineffective.

The macaque monkeys of Japan feed on sweet potatoes which they dig up; usually they eat them as they are, and have to put up with the earth still clinging to them. However, one monkey was seen washing a sweet potato in the water before eating it; after that all the horde to which it belonged started to wash its potatoes. Similarly, in Britain, there are small birds who have learned to take the tops off milk bottles in order to drink their contents.

When we reach the highest levels in the evolution of behaviour, we find species the individuals of which show signs of serious disturbance if they are isolated. In this respect dogs, for example, are on a par with the superior primates; when adult, a dog brought up in isolation is incapable of sexual behaviour. The great apes in zoos are so disturbed by their situation that there is very little reproduction. Moreover, it is at this level of anthropoids that self-awareness appears; thus a baboon with a metallic spot on its face did not react in front of a mirror, while a gorilla did.

Modes of cultural transmission reach a superior level when cultural transmission is no longer achieved solely by imitation, but also by other means: communication, language, words. This stage begins to appear among the superior primates.

Human behaviour and culture

The essential characteristic of the human race is the degree to which its culture has developed. Not only has behaviour been developed culturally, in a way to which the use of words has made a major contribution, but all knowledge can similarly be transmitted in words, these words being extended by the use of written signs and by numerous codes of communication. With man, culture changes scale: it invades everything. That happens to such a degree that the cultural element can prevail over various physiological, anatomical and even genetic factors.

This has been demonstrated by the remarkable results of the study and treatment of children born hermaphrodite as a result of a hormone accident (made by John Money). In all cases these children have almost the same starting point. Some have been brought up as girls and others as boys, and have undergone treatment adequate enough for them to be able to find a role in society and lead an almost normal life in the sex in which they have been brought up. The conditions for success depend largely on the quality of the child's family circle and confirmation of the sex that has been chosen; any doubts cast later on this sex, for example at puberty, lead to grave disturbances. Sexual reorientation, even in opposition to the genetic sex, can thus be carried through provided that it is started before the age of two. That shows us how much the cultural element predominates in the construction of human conduct. Here the sociological aspect of sex can be realized even at the opposite pole to the three other aspects which are usually determinative: chromosomic sex, anatomical sex and physiological sex. That does not mean that sex is insignificant or neutral, since the choice of sex is absolutely necessary and any questioning of it is disastrous. This example is not intended to encourage pointless experiments, but is simply meant to demonstrate the magnitude of the cultural element, and particularly education, in the realization of human behaviour. In the same way, the Kinsey Report shows that human sexual behaviour is influenced by surrounding culture in the same way as language or clothing.

Thus the numerous non-genetic elements which serve to establish human behaviour tell against any claim that this behaviour is totally determined by genes; this is true, moreover, not only of man, but also of the vertebrates. However, the fact that a pattern of behaviour is not entirely determined by the genes does not mean that it is completely free of all determinism. Thus such behaviour can be inhibited, or provoked, by physiological factors. These factors, often genetically programmed, can also depend on non-genetic determinants; in that case they constitute a non-genetic element in the formation of behaviour which can subject it to a more or less strict determinism, giving rise to a more or less narrow margin of behaviour that is not determined. For all that, one cannot claim that there is no such thing as a genetic inheritance in matters of behaviour. In fact, each individual has tendencies which to a large degree are without doubt hereditary: these tendencies exist even when they are not expressed in behaviour, because they are controlled or repressed. Moreover, vast though the possibilities of the human individual are, they are limited by his or her genetic constitution; even if our particular mode of behaviour exploits only one part of these possibilities, it is undeniable that we often come up against the limits of our organic and intellectual resources.

Self-construction and purpose in human behaviour. Freedom

This leads us to the notion of human behaviour as being essentially built up by the individual and by the society in which he or she lives, clearly using the resources that are organically available. Because society plays a part in the construction of behaviour, this behaviour has to be patterned on models. Because the individual constructs his or her own behaviour patterns, he or she has to make a choice between different models and to have the means of assimilating them.

The rejection of models suggested by the environment produces an illusion of doing without models and thus in reality amounts to a choice of counter-models (this rejection may be prompted by the inadequacy of the models put forward).

The way in which the individual constructs his or her behaviour inevitably arises from the choices by which he or she favours certain possibilities from among the vast array available. Clearly that is only possible because of the previous existence (and substantial development) of the acquired behaviour, particularly of

The human being cannot survive and develop normally without learning a culture.

Photo Pfaltzer- Viollet

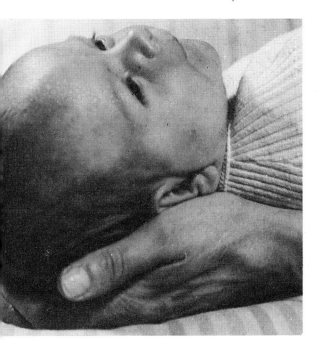

culture. These choices call for a sense of purpose in behaviour, which can be seen from the way in which it is organized. This sense of purpose can already be found among numerous vertebrates, where different kinds of behaviour can be prompted by a major drive within the individual: the search for food, self-preservation, reproduction. The motivation provided by such a sense is often used in the study of learning processes, for example to test the capacities of an animal which is trying to get food. However, this purposive behaviour remains temporary and is limited to the period during which it is being prompted by a particular drive. This is only a partial sense of purpose, and is more apparent than real.

By contrast, human behaviour can be orientated on a sense of purpose which is not just fragmentary, but overall, relating to long periods and even to an entire lifetime, taking the form of long-term planning. Such a capacity implies, first, that the subject is conscious, informed about the environment and about his or her own potentialities. This awareness, the sense of purpose which guides choices and the effective implementation of purposive behaviour, is the essential feature of the freedom which is the impulse behind all self-constructed behaviour. Granted, human beings are given numerous conditioned reflexes and undergo various learning processes during their existence. But they differ from other mammals in their self-awareness: they provide themselves with their own conditioned reflexes and patterns of learning (if certain individuals fail to do this, they suffer as a result). Contrary to other mammals, the human being with an overriding sense of purpose can transcend the most powerful drives like the need for food or self-preservation (and, more easily, sexual urges).

The problem which thus arises for the individual – as for human societies – is that of the choice of the final purpose of forms of behaviour. This problem necessarily issues in an ethic, the role of which is to illuminate the value of the goals which are aimed at, the real motives behind the choice, and to ensure coherence

Human beings are capable of conceiving of a kind of existence which goes beyond their present state.
Photo Roger-Viollet

between types of behaviour and their final goal. Without going into the details of ethics, we can note that an evolutionary perspective calls for goals which represent an advance on the existing state. In fact, human beings are capable of conceiving of a type of existence which transcends their existing state. At least from historical times, philosophies and religions – and for that matter stories and popular legends – have directed human beings towards a state superior to that which they know, or even towards beings presented as much superior to themselves. It is from the perspective of an increase of human potentialities, of the capacity for constructing one's own behaviour, the capacity for freedom, that the least alienating, the least limiting ethic is framed. This ethic aims at the greatest freedom for the human being, by putting forward the loftiest and broadest goals imaginable. Human beings have reached a stage of cultural development where it is possible for them to conceive and pursue such perspectives without waiting for the very uncertain possibility of their realization through a future biological evolution.

Changes in human freedom

The fact that human behaviour is constructed through its social setting does not necessarily imply that it is constructed by the individual, although this self-construction is possible in a social framework. One can even envisage the self-construction being hindered by the generalized imposition of preconceived social models. Such a situation maims the capacity of the human individual to construct his or her own behaviour, destroys his freedom and does not in any way correspond to real social needs. Even short of such totalitarian constraints, it often happens that an environment to which an individual has not been adapted more or less hampers the construction of behaviour.

On the other hand, it can happen that the individual rejects the capacity for having a sense of purpose, by refusing it. In these conditions, various tendencies or drives can make the imperative rules of behaviour to which the individual is subjected less important: these tendencies are no longer controlled by choices nor guided by a plan; they lead to an alienation of the individual by the determining factors which call forth and stimulate his or her tendencies or drives. In that case behaviour is no longer constructed by the self but from outside and lacks unity or direction; it comes about through passive adherence to models which are imposed from outside and not chosen in accordance with an ultimate aim. This rejection of a free and responsible human condition is rarely explicit: it more often appears in the form of a demand for a 'freedom' which is generally left undefined.

However, a careful examination of the function of this alleged freedom shows that it consists in following tendencies and obeying impulses without reserve, refusing to be subject to the control of that sense of purpose which alone allows the self to construct a coherent pattern of behaviour (this sense of purpose may well be rejected as 'constraining'). The result of such an attitude is to plunge the individual back into a blind determinism from which human beings had emerged after a long period of evolution, and thereafter it is very firmly subjected to that determinism. There are bulimic brains which can no longer suppress the desire to eat and are subject to the semi-reflexes of consuming food; there are eroticized brains enslaved by the need for sexual fulfilment; in a similar way many other uncontrolled human needs can take on an exclusive and determinative importance for behaviour. This determinism reduces – and can even destroy – freedom by governing human behaviour in accordance with automatic patterns which re-establish the ascendancy of organic and instinctual factors, to the detriment of cultural development. Such a regression in the human individual towards conduct imitative of instinctual behaviour makes him or her out of phase with the evolutionary stage of the species, and particularly the social life which makes up humanity. This produces conflicts and disorder in human societies, whereas animal societies benefit from automatic regulative factors relatively independent of individual initiatives (which are restricted).

Alienated and conditioned human behaviour is sufficiently frequent for some people to be tempted to see it as the rule and to reduce humanity to these dimensions. In fact, such behaviour does not in any way make up the whole of human behaviour; it is not even the most characteristic type, which must be identified by real possibilities and not by possibilities mutilated in various ways.

This survey of the evolution of behaviour from the simplest animals to humanity therefore shows us man as the culmination of a process of liberating the individual subject from the organic constraints which are a necessary consequence or his or her existence. Such liberation corres-

ponds to a faculty of self-determination, of the conscious construction of an individual behaviour, his or her personal choices; these constitute the freedom of each person and also

Sociobiology

The first scientific works which led to this theory were mathematical; calculations were made beginning from what were considered to be probable hypotheses, about how selection would function and what results it would lead to. These calculations produce what is called a mathematical 'model' and are part of a scientific discipline called 'model-making'. To begin with, a biological model applied to biology is no more than a hypothesis; it is not a scientific fact. When the observed results, in nature or experience, agree with the predictions of the model, this confirms the hypothesis presented by the model, given that the agreement cannot be attributed to other mechanisms (possibly unknown). The fact of observing one agreement does not prove much: several agreements are needed for it to be possible to say that the hypothesis has been verified in a significant way, provided that there are not as many conflicting factors.

The first models in sociobiology were presented by the Englishman W. D. Hamilton in 1964, to explain how the 'altruistic' behaviour of the workers among social insects, for example bees, favoured the selection of their immediate relatives ('kin selection') and thus gave added opportunity to the 'altruistic' gene, consequently furthering the development of social life. In 1975, an American, E. O. Wilson (a specialist in ants), produced a large work on 'sociobiology', described as a 'new synthesis'. A number of works, above all from the Anglo-Saxon world, then contributed towards making the sociobiological theory extremely fashionable. It was applied to all kinds of animals and of course to human beings, to take account of social evolution; it took as its basis the automatic occurrence of a selection favouring the 'altruistic' gene.

These sociobiological models are ingenious, and are extremely interesting to the degree that they are confirmed by certain observations. Unfortunately, those who defend the theory have often retained the favourable examples and neglected the unfavourable ones, which their opponents unfailingly bring up in order to contradict them. One might remember that some examples in connection with wasps and ants seem to fit in with the theory well, to the extent that automatic behaviour is well developed in these groups (that might simplify various explanations). However, that is not generally the case, and other examples contradict the theory. The sociobiologists react to obstacles to their theory by adjusting it through the addition of new hypotheses which reconcile the calculations with the observed results. With the complications introduced by successive corrections, this theory could end up a long way from its starting point (as also happened with the theory of evolution).

Numerous ethologists regard the expression 'altruistic gene' as an illegitimate simplification. Of course the term 'altruistic' is not taken to attribute a specific intention to the insect: only the result of its activity is an advantage for 'the other', behaviour being controlled by the genes. However, the very notion of altruism would seem to be an excessive simplification, since there are very different ways of behaving to the advantage of others, depending on the species. The types of behaviour in question usually depend not on one gene but on an unknown number of more or less independent genes – probably a large one; of course, none of the genes presupposed here is known at present, either in formal genetics (the study of heredity between parents and children) or molecu-

define his or her responsibilities. So this freedom does not end up in anarchic and random behaviour, but in a purposive orientation of individual behaviour on long-term projects, plans in which men and women express their boundless aspirations.

By returning to palaeontology and prehistory, we shall try to define as clearly as possible what pointers the past gives us towards the process of attaining this freedom.

We shall then examine the message addressed to men and women as free beings by the Bible, when it speaks of their origins.

lar genetics (the study of the biochemical composition of the gene and its functioning). Even in its best examples, the sociobiological theory remains a hypothesis, sometimes an attractive hypothesis, which can have the merit of stimulating certain research into the social insects.

When this theory is extrapolated to superior animals, like birds, mammals and man, it resorts to extreme simplification, and scientific certainty dissolves in a flood of accumulated hypotheses. It is a trite remark to point out that every long-range extrapolation is an error in logic which leads to extremely doubtful results. Similarly, in the case of man, the effective context of behaviour, the choice made in a cultural setting from a wide range of possibilities, limits the role of one gene or another so that it only determines a 'tendency', usually for the most part controllable in terms of these intentions of the subject which are actually put into practice.

However, the interest of the sociobiologist has also become political; this increases his notoriety to the detriment of his strictly scientific value. For often ideological foundations determine whether the theory is accepted or rejected. That explains the passionate struggles which develop over this issue. The members of a society which would seek to shape the behaviour of the individual entirely reject the sociobiological model on principle. At the opposite extreme, the sociobiologist is held up as a champion of science by those who support a human élitism based on the genetic superiority of some over others (and often implying a right of the superior over the inferior for the good of the species). The political exploitation of science has often given rise to this kind of abuse.

61

4

The Emergence of Man and the Problems of Hominization

The emergence of man, 'hominization', is the result of an evolution in anatomical and mental structures which in essentials is spread over the last four million years.

During the course of this period, both processes of evolution have developed jointly but with different rhythms:

The *anatomical evolution* is the more remote one; the essential transformations had already been realized a million years ago (*homo erectus*) and some of the major innovations took place even earlier (the Australopitheci).

The *mental evolution* came later; the major acquisitions have appeared over the last million years.

While it is now possible to trace the main lines of the anatomical evolution of the hominids, it is far more difficult to follow the evolution of their behaviour. The explicit evidence of mental activity is still scant, above all for the early periods. On the other hand the arguments derived from palaeontology (the volume of the brain, its structure as far as this can be determined from endocasts, and so on) are sometimes equivocal (cf. the discussion on language in connection with Neanderthal man). However, it is possible to posit certain stages in the evolution of behaviour. We shall find them within the three major evolutionary stages (the 'human strata') represented by the Australopitheci, *homo erectus* and *homo sapiens*.

The Australopitheci and *homo habilis*

This group of hominids, so far known only in southern and eastern Africa, comprises various forms whose phylogenetic history (i.e. the relationship between their different branches) extends over at least three million years and has led to numerous discussions, constantly fed by new discoveries. Here we shall only present the basic features of this history.

The earliest Australopitheci appeared about four million years ago: they were discovered in East Africa (the region of the Afars in Ethiopia and Tanzania). These are the earliest forms, of which the skeleton of 'Lucy', almost complete (Afars, about 3 Ma), offers a good illustration (*australopithecus afarensis*). No trace of any artefact has yet been found in association with these early forms. The acquisition of an upright position, walking on two legs, is irrefutably attested by the discovery of traces of footprints preserved on a bed of hardened ash dated between 3.6 and 3.8 Ma (Laetoli in Tanzania).

Between about 3 and 2.2 Ma, Australopitheci apparently corresponding to a single form (*australopithecus africanus*) are attested in southern and eastern Africa.

Between 2.2 and 1.6 Ma, on the other hand, the group becomes differentiated in a spectacular way. We find:

1. The persistence of a gracile form of Australopithecus, probably related to the previous kind, but in a more advanced stage of evolution. It is known only in East Africa.

2. About 2.2. Ma, a 'bestial' form, *australopithecus robustus*, appeared. This is represented, with regional variations, in southern and eastern Africa. This form survived until about a million years ago without ever seeming to have attained a higher mental level (no artefacts are associated with it).

3. About 1.6 to 1.8 Ma forms appeared with cranial capacities (about 750 cc) clearly superior on average to those of previous forms (about 450 cc). There is agreement today that these should be distinguished from the Australopitheci and should be recognized as the first representatives of the genus *homo* (*homo habilis*).

Thus the history of this first stratum of hominids, which we can follow for more than two million years, shows a burgeoning evolution from beings of a small size (1.2 metres) who already walked on two feet; some branches lead to man (*homo habilis*), while others find themselves led into dead ends (for example, *australopithecus robustus*).

The first artefacts which can be recognized with certainty date from between 2.3 and 2.5 Ma. So in the present state of our knowledge they are much later than the appearance of the first Australopitheci known to us, but later than *homo habilis*. They take the form of flakes of rock produced deliberately and pebbles cut in a rudimentary way (pebble culture); there is only a very limited number of different types.

The first domestic structures, consisting of a collection of large stones in a regular arrangement (traces of the ground-plans of rudimentary huts) go back to about 2 Ma.

The following facts should be remembered in connection with the history of behaviour:

1. Attainment of an upright position (before about 3.8 Ma) seems to have largely preceded the spread of the making of artefacts. This displacement in time is perhaps due to a gap in our present knowledge; much more probably it illustrates the length of time needed to profit effectively from the attainment of an upright position.

2. The artefact represents the first implementation of a plan. It presupposes an anticipation of the result of an action (the realization of an idea, followed by utilization and the result). This gives us the first indication of a degree of detachment in activities. At this stage anticipation must have been of short duration, and the artefact will have been abandoned directly after use. Furthermore, pebble culture would appear to be extraordinarily stereotyped. Any evolution it displays in the course of the million and a half years of its

existence will have been very slow. The capacity for innovation remained very weak. It is thought that in the very first stages of pebble culture anticipation could have been limited to the choice of pebbles providing a natural and suitable surface (this is the problem of the limitation of the tools used, but not made, by the great anthropoid apes).

3. Domestic structures are worth noting for two reasons:

– They are evidence of a certain form of social organization (community life; organization of hunting and other activities).

– Where we have places lived in for a long time, these arrangements also bear witness to the capacity of a social group to plan a project (the relatively long time needed to make a hut, with a view to the exploitation of the environment: hunting, gathering, a source of water, sharing food, etc.). These social structures argue in favour of the existence of a certain level of communication (language) from the Australopithecan stage on.

The group of *homo erectus*

This was widespread throughout the ancient world (Asia, Africa and Europe) for almost a million years. The different forms known to us, Pithecanthropos, Sinanthropos, Atlanthropos and so on, represent either geographical variants or different stages of evolution. This is easily conceivable because of the large area of dissemination and the longevity of the species. These were individuals of medium height (about 1.5 m) and with a cranial capacity of between about 860 and 1280 cc. Their anatomical organization is not basically different from that of modern man. *Homo erectus* is without doubt a descendant of *homo habilis*. His affinity to what are thought to be the first forms of *homo sapiens* allows virtually no doubt on that point.

Several important innovations may be stressed in connection with the evolution of behaviour:

1. In terms of *artefacts*. The appearance, about 700,000 years ago, of the handaxe, which developed out of pebble culture (the transition came about, for example, through utensils of an Abbevillian kind). This implement, much more elaborate than the pebble tool, is characterized by the discovery of regularity and symmetry (stones with the shape of a heart or an almond) and by an increase in the 'usable surface' of the object. So this is a simultaneous first discovery of both aesthetics and efficiency. The care taken in the making of the tool presupposes prolonged anticipation. One can already envisage the symbolism involved. The implement is made without there being any direct spatial and temporal relationship with the satisfaction of the need which is to come (cf. the elaborate techniques used to treat wood and bone, using fire, etc.). The tool was clearly made with a purpose.

The development of the technique of building up an implement from a basic nucleus is at the same time a good illustration of the extension of the project in time. Here we have the preparation of the basic nucleus, the preparation of the implement, and its possible use. However, one is struck by the uniformity of handaxe factories throughout the ancient world. Moreover any evolution to be found in them over the course of time is still very slow in relation to the period of time under consideration (about 600,000 years). Innovation remains very limited (what we have is essentially the transmission of acquired skills and little individual acquisition).

2. *Fire*. This has been used and kept going since about 700,000 years ago (Vertezöllös in Hungary, Terra amata near Nice and later Chou-kou-tien in China). While it may not be enough to characterize man, at least it distinguishes him from the rest of the animal world. It is significant in several respects:

(a) Keeping fire going presupposes that the habitat has a considerable degree of stability (Chou-kou-tien) and that as a result the social structures are equally stable (common interests);

(b) Fire has a significance comparable to that of

Prehistoric Acheulean herth at Terra Amata (France). Collection Musée de lk'Homme. *Photo H. de Lumley*

the tool to the degree that it presupposes an anticipation of need. It provides an external development of a vital function (cooking, digestion), just as the stone tool supplements the tusk or the claw;

(c) It increases control of the external milieu (protection against the rigours of cold, defence against wild animals, an end to total subjection to the night, and so on).

3. *Cannibalism*. This is not to be thought of as an alimentary practice. The widening of the occipital orifice practised on several skulls of Sinanthropos in Peking, probably with the aim of eating the brains, has been considered the first manifestation of ritual (about 300,000 years ago?). Even at the risk of being proved wrong,

we should probably regard this practice as the first recognizable sign of the metaphysical preoccupation of humanity.

Such rites, still practised by certain populations today, were aimed at appropriating the physical or intellectual qualities of the dead person (as were the majority of acts of cannibalism). If the comparison holds, it implies that the *homo erectus* of Chou-kou-tien was capable of discerning intellectual values and placing himself in a hierarchy *vis-à-vis* these values (that is to say, appropriating the qualities of the strongest, of the one more 'cunning' than he, and so on).

Homo sapiens

The distinction between *homo erectus* and the first *homo sapiens* is conventional enough; without doubt the transition was gradual and remains difficult to fix with any certainty, given the very small number of bone remains that we have. The first *homo sapiens* probably appeared between 300,000 and 400,000 years ago. In Europe, the primitive forms, whose membership of the 'club' *sapiens* was only accepted quite recently (Swanscombe man, Steinheim man, and so on) evolved towards a specialized type, Neanderthal man (*homo sapiens neanderthalensis*), who appeared more than 100,000 years ago (France, Belgium, Spain, Italy, etc.) and disappeared 30,000 years ago. Other branches which gave birth to *homo sapiens sapiens* probably developed partly in the area around the Mediterranean (notably the Near East) and partly in the East. Those in the area around the Mediterranean definitively supplanted Neanderthal man some 30,000 years ago.

1. *Artefacts* underwent a considerable evolution. Techniques of preparation prior to the making of tools were developed; they became more diversified and specialized, getting lighter and more efficient; and the projectile, which marks the beginning of a liberation from spatial restrictions, made a first appearance (from about 100,000 years ago), etc.

2. The appearance of *burial places and funeral rites* connected with the idea of a life beyond (organization of a response to the problem of death) appear about 70,000 years ago (La-Chapelle-aux-Saints, France). It is interesting to see these practices appearing with *homo sapiens neanderthalensis*, whose archaic character has long been exaggerated (particular anatomical characteristics, no signs of artistic skill). Cannibalism persists.

3. Very elaborate *works of art* appeared with *homo sapiens sapiens* about 28,000 years ago (for instance in France and Russia), reaching a climax in Europe about 20,000 to 15,000 years ago (at Lascaux in the Dordogne, France). From the very beginning, this art is not archaic or 'naive'. It first of all bears witness to a remarkable mastery. The art is generally accepted as having had essentially a magical function, being an aspect of the elaboration of myths (as, for example, in the caves of the Dordogne, cf. the work of André Leroi-Gourhan) rather than being for realistic anecdotal representation.

Wall paintings have virtually no portrayals of human beings; nor are they a bestiary. They are subject to rigorous organization governed by complex symbolism (a balance of male and female 'values'). In many cases these paintings have been done in places which are obscure or difficult to find; this rules out a simple preoccupation with decoration.

The 'Venus' sculptures suggest even more clearly the role of art as material support in the elaboration and propagation of myths (fertility, etc.).

However, the frequency with which artefacts (needles, harpoons, sticks, pendants) are decorated needs to be stressed; it is not clear whether or not this should be seen as evidence of a simple aesthetic preoccupation (appearance of a sense of 'beauty').

This essentially symbolic and mythical palaeolithic art disappeared at the end of the glacial period (the end of the Magdalenian period, about 10,000 years ago) without any direct descendants.

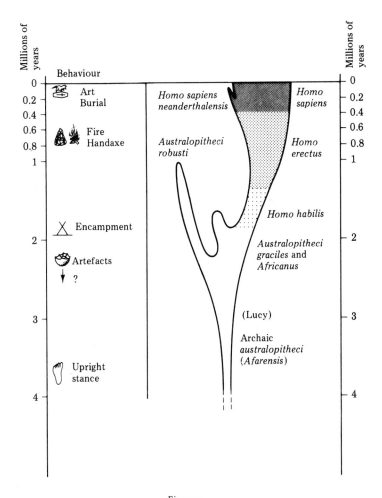

Figure 9
The human branch from its ancestors, the Australopitheci, to the present day (some scholars place *australopithecus africanus* in the 'robust' branch; others make *africanus* the common strain of the 'robust' branch and *homo habilis*).

67

The wall paintings of the Spanish Levant and Africa which come next in time have a quite different style and different conceptions. Human figures abound here in compositions which are scenes of everyday life (hunting, war, gathering, collecting honey, etc.); they apparently have no mythical significance.

It is possible that from this period on (mesolithic and neolithic period) 'speech' was sufficiently elaborate for art no longer to be the main channel for the expression of myths. In the mesolithic period art is progressively schematized, moving in the direction of writing which was coming into being during the course of the neolithic period, when a new art was to appear.

Figure 9 gives a synthetic representation of the evolution of the human branch. Estimations of duration are rather shorter than they recently used to be. Obviously there will be further growth in our knowledge in the future.

The cradle of humanity

There has been much discussion as to the geographical setting, if not of the first human beings, at least of the first representatives of the evolutionary branch which led up to man. This cradle of humanity has been moved around, depending on where fossils have been found. Having left Europe where Neanderthal man was discovered, it moved to Asia to meet up with Pithecanthropos and Sinanthropos. It seems to have paused for the moment in Africa, among the Australopitheci. Will it start moving again in the wake of new discoveries? Some years ago, Abbé Breuil commented that it was more like a perambulator. However, the Australopitheci seem to be the originators of the human form and, up to the present, remains of Australopitheci have only been found in a limited region of southern and eastern Africa. It now remains to discover the geographical spread of the ancestors of the Australopitheci; however, the identity of these ancestors is still the subject of vigorous discussion.

Polyphyletism and monophyletism

Did humanity derive from just one couple? This question is bound up with that of the geographical setting of the cradle of humanity. Obviously, if humanity descended from just one couple, that couple would be very localized, but there would be virtually no chance of our being able to identify it or to say precisely where it was located. However, the question does arise above all in connection with the modes of evolution by which new species are formed, modes which are called speciations. What we know of speciations today sheds some scientific light on this problem (see the box on Speciation, p.72).

All the animal species were formed from ancestors who evolved more or less rapidly, most often diversifying in the process. Contrary to what we sometimes find with plants, it is very improbable that an animal species could emerge from the convergence and fusion of several ancestral species. The general rule is that the animal species diversify, giving rise to divergent branches which can become so many distinct species (the process of cladogenesis), separated from one another without hope of ever being fused together again. Such an evolution ends up in some dispersion of new species, who adapt themselves to the changing conditions on earth and replace other species which have disappeared. It can equally happen that one species transforms itself into another species without becoming diversified (the process of anagenesis).

What essentially defines a species is the fact that its individuals are naturally fertile among themselves, whereas in nature the individuals of two different species do not normally interbreed. The resemblance between individuals of the same species is an evident consequence of their inter-fertility. The biological unity of the human species is now established by the total inter-fertility of all its geographical races. There would seem to be no way in which the species could have arisen from the fusion of several branches stemming from different species. We might suppose the human species as it is now to have derived from a single evolutionary phylum, and therefore to be a monophyletic species.

Of course, the human branch began to diversify before arriving at present-day man. We might ask whether certain branches of this strain produced human beings of another species which have now disappeared. This question was already raised in connection with Neanderthal man, but the Neanderthalians are now included in the species of *homo sapiens*. It seems, rather, that the whole of the human branch, from the Australopitheci to *homo sapiens*, underwent a general transformation following the same evolutionary direction (anagenesis), preserving its specific unity; this does not preclude the early existence of geographical races within our species. The polyphyletic theories are often based on an under-estimation of the time needed to form new species and an over-estimation of the apparent differences between fossils of the human line. Formed at the time of a mainly descriptive palaeontology, they do not fit in with studies of evolutionary biology.

Polygenism, monogenism

Polygenism is the hypothesis according to which the human species will have originated from a more or less extended population (or several related populations) which will have evolved progressively towards its present state.

Monogenism is the hypothesis according to which the human species will have derived from a single original couple (this hypothesis is also called 'Adamic'). Such an original couple could have emerged – by major mutations – from earlier non-human beings which themselves will have constituted a population.

All the species now known to us appear in the form of populations. Even those 'unknown species' whose existence is accepted (the Yeti, the giant octopus) are considered to have derived from at least one population. The majority of mechanisms for speciation known to us involve populations. This is the case with geo-graphical speciation (also known as allopatric, because it is based on the separation of habitats). Two populations, originally identical, are subsequently separated by an obstacle (geographical or climatic); they evolve differently by diverging from one another until they constitute two species which do not interbreed and are definitively separated. There are also instances where the separation of the two populations is not the result of a geographical obstacle but of an ecological or behavioural difference ('sympatric' speciations, because the two new species have the same native habitat).

The differences between the two future species are produced by mutations, possibly then selected in different ways depending on the native habitat, the ecological environment, behaviour, and so on. The concept of speciation by evolution of populations is now the one most widely accepted by biologists. It has the advantage of putting the origin of species in a situation resembling that of present-day life as it pursues its evolution.

However, one could also imagine that one species went through the initial stage of a unique couple deriving from parents of another neighbouring species. Once this couple had produced an increasingly numerous population of descendants, the single-couple phase would be far enough in the background to pass generally unnoticed. Such a speciation would be of the sympatric type since it was achieved in one place, the new and the old species living in the same habitat. Moreover, it would be the result of a sufficiently important mutation for the new species no longer to be able to cross with the old.

Is this hypothesis of a speciation by a unique couple a real possibility? What is its probability?

The formation of one new species from another, like the division of a hereditary branch into two new species, involves the realization of reproductive isolation between the two species concerned. That means that these species can no longer cross in nature, can no longer produce common descendants. This reproductive isolation is based on genetic differences, i.e. on mutations. For it to be achieved directly in an individual, either a group of simultaneous mutations affecting this individual, or one very great mutation, would be needed. Each of these possibilities is extremely slender, since they involve mutations affecting either the genes or the chromosomes (see the box on Speciation, p.72).

It is generally supposed that such mutations tend to come about more in the form of re-arrangements or mutations of chromosomes which modify the location of the genes in the chromosomes. In fact these mutations of chromosomes do very often make it relatively difficult for hybrids from two different forms to appear. Moreover, we know that quite a number of them can be found in the line of human descent: at least ten of them are known to divide man from the great anthropoid apes. However, of itself a mutation of chromosomes does not generally bring about reproductive isolation: it is usually found in a population in which mutants continue to cross with others: the relative difficulty of hybridation consists simply in a reduction of fertility in hybrids. Isolation usually comes about only through the combination of several mutations of chromosomes accumulated over the course of time (to which mutations of genes are often added).

Suppose, nevertheless, that a very great mutation, in genes or chromosomes, by itself resulted in a reproductive isolation. This rare event could succeed only if it simultaneously affected the two homologous chromosomes in such a way that they both carried the mutation (we in fact know that the chromosomes make up two homologous series, one coming from the mother and the other from the father). The achievement of such a match is obviously rarer than the event affecting a single chromosome (the square of the probability). Moreover, for the event effectively to produce a new species, it would have to take place at the same time and in the same location in two individuals of complementary sexes, so that a father and a mother could generate the new branch. Such a combination would be extremely rare.

These very faint probabilities are slightly increased if we take account of the size of the population of Australopitheci (which has been estimated as being under a million individuals) and the number of successive generations open to the event (perhaps at most 50,000 over a million years). The event in question still remains very improbable.

One could certainly suppose that mutagens will have increased the probability of mutations at certain periods, in proportions which it is difficult to specify, but the mutations produced experimentally by such agents are for the most part weak and generally detrimental rather than sources of evolutionary progress.

Of course, just because an event is highly improbable, it does not mean that it is impossible, but one can well understand that scientists do not readily invoke such events unless they have irrefutable proof of them.

A religious person could dream of amazing miracles by which God would manifest himself to humanity in exceptional circumstances. However, we should not forget that these miracles would have to be addressed to conscious beings, men and women, capable of appreciating their miraculous character. Hominization necessarily preceded the existence of these conscious beings and would not be a sign addressed to them; it would relate, rather, to the inexorable development of the creative process, sufficiently coherent to dispense with a specific supplementary intervention.

So if we need not necessarily rule out completely the possibility that humanity originated from just one couple, it is more probable, in the light of current knowledge (incomplete though it may be), that this origin should be sought in a population. The dimensions of this population could have been more or less limited or extended (a clan, tribe, people, group of peoples). At all events, the monophyletism of the human species calls for the existence, at a certain period in its evolution, of one population, the ancestors of all those to come. However, this single population could not yet have been human, since hominization developed later over a group of populations.

Hominization and its place in time

The present state of our knowledge allows us to locate with varying degrees of precision a number of stages in the development of human intelligence. These stages are only points of reference, arbitrary breaks, in a continuous development (at least to outward appearance).

There is no simple reply to the question which naturally comes to mind: 'From what point are human beings human?' This is because the question introduces limits, classifications, into a continuous process. On the other hand, it must be noted that of all living beings, man is the only one to have a double identity card.

Like all other species, man can be identified by a group of anatomical characteristics peculiar to himself, or which he shares with other forms of the same branch (the same phylum). Man, an integral part of the living world, can be included in zoological classifications in the same way as a beetle or a fly.

Alone of all living forms, he can be identified by his intellectual faculties. *Homo* is *sapiens*. That is the utter originality of hominization.

So when we ask the question, 'From what point are human beings human?', we must be quite specific about the identity with which we are concerned.

Anatomical man, *homo anatomicus*, is without doubt very ancient. He has probably existed for more than three million years. We recognize him as a biped with hands; his jaws have no teeth and his skull, balanced on the vertebral column, disengaged from the muscles which constrained it, is beginning to house an increasingly large brain.

That is a portrait of the Australopitheci, the first beings who will have combined in themselves the essential anatomical features of man. On the other hand, what we know of their behaviour suggests mental structures which do not have the essential attributes of human thought: the predominance of repetitive acts, short-term purpose in operations, and so on. That can be inferred from the fact that over millions of years their manufacturing process remained relatively stable, without decisive progress.

However, that is no excuse for a revival of the polemic formerly prompted by the Australopitheci: man or monkey? Not being fully human does not mean being a monkey. We must get used to the idea that humanity has come from a line which has evolved while producing progressive signs of hominization; that does not allow us to specify the exact date of hominization and the physical state of being hominized. We may suppose that there was a specific moment of hominization which we cannot establish, the result of an important mutation. This moment can also be envisaged as having been extended in time, without any very striking events.

Going back into the past, this human line meets up with common ancestors and the species which are closest to it: the great anthropoid apes. This stage of separation between the human and the anthropoid lines is put at different periods by different specialists.

The palaeontologist is familiar with these problems, which we come up against once more, for example, in connection with the first birds or the first mammals; however, it is far more difficult to discover the first sparks of reflective thought than the traces of the first feathers or the first fur.

To sum up, we may say that in all probability the beginnings of a human form preceded the human mind.

Metaphysical man, with whom we identify, can be recognized from long-term purposive acts which do not produce immediate returns, and ultimately from gratuitous acts. The more long-term the project, the more man leaves open the possibility of choice. The criterion of choice, of freedom of choice, is a basic feature of the man we seek.

We have seen that evidences of behaviour like the handaxe, fire, ritual cannibalism, are so many phenomena in which there is no simple and immediate relationship between cause and effect. These actions are so many traces which

Speciation

This is the stage of evolution in which new species come about. A common error is to suppose that a single mutation habitually produces a new species. This idea is manifestly false, since it would lead to making each human being – apart from identical twins – an original species; in fact every human being differs from his or her neighbour or brother or sister, not only by one but by several mutations.

Usually a certain number of accumulated genetic differences are needed to separate two sister species from the same ancestral species. These genetic differences could be either mutations modifying a gene or the rearrangement (or mutation) of chromosomes, modifying the disposition of genes in the chromosomes without affecting the constitution of these genes.

In order for there to be speciation, it is necessary for the differences between the two forms which have become two species to be such that these forms cannot exchange genes between themselves, i.e. that together, in nature, they can no longer produce hybrids capable of living and reproducing. The fact that breeders or growers often succeed in *artificially* producing hybrids of two different species in laboratory conditions does not mean that evolution has not really separated these two species which, in nature, do not interbreed.

Several forms of speciation are known, and attempts are made to describe new examples.

Geographical – or allopatric – speciation (in two different native habitats) is the best known. It begins when a single population is divided into two by a natural barrier arising out of climatic variations (glaciers) or geographical variations (an arm of the sea or a mountain). During this separation, each of the two parts evolves differently from the other, because of mutations which undergo divergent selections; if the separation lasts for long enough, the two divergent evolutions end up by producing two groups which have become incapable of interbreeding naturally. Among animals as we know them there are examples of species which to begin with were separated geographically by the quaternary glaciations, became different species during this separation, and then met up again when the geographical barrier disappeared. At that point they proved incapable of natural interbreeding. By preventing them from exchanging genes, the prolonged geographical separation favoured the divergent evolution of their species.

Sympatric speciations (i.e. speciations in the same native habitat) are not favoured by these circumstances: the two species in process of separating constantly run the risk of becoming mixed, which could compromise their separation. Their only chance of separation is if the first differences which distinguish them tend to prevent them from crossing. For example, these first differences could impel them towards two slightly different modes of life (ecological separation) which would partially prevent them from mixing genetically. Or again, the first differences might introduce slightly different mating customs (ethological separation), which would impel individuals to choose a partner from their group rather than the other, and that would partly avoid genetic mixing. Finally, the first differences could be rearrangements of chromosomes, of such a kind that hybrids between the two future species were at a disadvantage (in general because their fertility was lowered). If some rearrangements of chromosomes were successively accumulated, one could end up after a certain period with two true species, hybrids between which were completely sterile. That would totally prevent genetic mixing.

In general, these differences in chromosomes would appear only in half measure (that is to say in one chromosome of two similar ones) in an initial individual who continued to be part of the mother species. The successive descendants of this individual could accumulate the difference so that eventually it affected both chromosomes, and that could lead them to form an original group which tended to isolate itself from the rest of the species, ultimately evolving into a different species. All this tends to tell against populations with a fairly large number of individuals.

The term systemic speciation is used to denote what primarily isolates the mutants from the original populations. Such speciations are inevitably very rare, given that the chances of effecting a mutation are small and that the chances of obtaining this same mutation simultaneously in a male and a female of the same population are that much smaller; moreover, it is often essential for the mutation to be achieved completely in the chromosomes (perhaps in two successive stages), and this diminishes further the chances of success. Finally, mutations which in themselves directly lead to total isolation are certainly very rare, since they are virtually unknown. Of course, the highly improbable is not the impossible, but one is not inclined to look for exceptional explanations to take account of natural phenomena.

Several examples of instantaneous speciations are known; these are speciations brought about in a particular way without any change in the genes of the chromosomes, but simply through polyploidization, that is to say, the multiplication of the number of chromosomes by two, three or more. In fact an individual with 4 n chromosomes (= tetraploid) and another with 2 n (normal individual = diploid) cannot together produce normal descendants: these are sterile and often not very viable. Several kinds of animal species are known which are formed in this way by the multiplication of the number of their chromosomes, but the phenomenon is rare and does not affect the human line nor that of apes in any way. Among plants, we know of examples of the instantaneous

formation of new species by the addition of the chromosomes of two or three neighbouring species; that is the case, for example, with cultivated wheat: obviously the human line and monkeys are not involved in any way with this phenomenon.

We can see that the essential result of speciation is to produce a break – a 'reproductive isolation' – between the two species which have been newly separated; these become groups of species evolving independently of each other, because there is no longer interbreeding, and therefore exchange of genes, between them.

This phenomenon can come about more or less quickly (or slowly) depending on circumstances: often thousands of years have been thought necessary in the case of geographical speciations. Several thousand years are perhaps enough when rearrangements of chromosomes are involved. Rather shorter lengths of time, some hundreds of years, are sometimes suggested, for example in the case of the genetic revolution thought to be behind the very rapid evolution of the fruit flies of Hawaii (but these flies can easily produce ten generations a year). The duration of speciation is only reduced to the period of a generation in the case of polyploidization (which does not concern either monkeys or human beings) or in the hypothetical cases of systemic speciation (a large mutation of genes or chromosomes). Over the course of the geological periods, palaeontologists often see that species remain stable for a long time and then undergo quite an evolutionary explosion. Some scientists have elevated that to a general rule, in the theory of 'punctuated equilibria': phases of long stability in species are followed by phases of almost instantaneous diversification. However, it should not be forgotten that, to a palaeontologist, 'instantaneous' can be anything from a thousand to a hundred thousand years, depending on the period in question.

indicate the existence of a long-term plan, a vision going beyond immediate utilitarianism to arrive at a symbolic understanding and a relationship with the invisible.

It seems very probable to us that the Pithecanthropi had acquired both identities, anatomical man and metaphysical man. The irony of history is that it was long doubted whether Pithecanthropos, *homo erectus*, walked on two feet. Nowadays he is generally accepted as having had a capacity for reflective thought, and the geneticists are no longer completely sure whether he formed a different biological species from *homo sapiens*.

Just as the Australopithecus gives us the first sketch of the human form, so *homo erectus* seems to bring the first sufficiently elaborate outline of thought. From that time on, the development of language allows a considerable amplification of social communication and the cultural transmission of acquired experiences. And these were transmitted durably, in space to contemporaries, and in time to other generations.

If one could quantify this evolution, which is not easy, there is no doubt that the curve would not show an arithmetical but a logarithmic progression (cf. Leroi-Gourhan's curve relating to the size of silex): the handaxe and the Apollo rocket are just two points on the same curve.

The growth of freedom: continuity or discontinuity?

This problem seems to us to be essentially metaphysical and theological.

The fossil evidence shows us human evolution as an apparently continuous process, represented by the existence of intermediate forms between the successive stages and by the polymorphism manifested by contemporary fossils, some being progressive and the others archaic.

That raises the problem of the continuity or discontinuity of the emergence of freedom, i.e. of the appearance of metaphysical man. This problem arises as we consider on the one hand hominization as a realization of the free being to a metaphysical (and theological) vocation, and on the other hand human speciation as the formation of the human biological species. We are adopting a metaphysical and theological perspective here since we are considering human freedom, but at the same time we must take account of possible scientific hypotheses about the formation of the human species. So we shall consider this problem from the perspective of faith, without neglecting its scientific aspects.

Acheulean handaxe (Somme). Lower palaeolithic period. Collection Musée de l'Homme.

Photo M. Delaplance

74

What would appear essential in the realization of free humanity is the fact that created beings are elevated to the rank of God's conversation partners. God speaks to them in a familiar way, treats them as responsible people and gives them responsibility, deals with them in relation to himself, in an eternal relationship of love. That implies attitudes, acts with a place in time and history, forming events and thus marking a historical and spiritual discontinuity. That is why it is natural for us to try to make the origin of this relationship of man as God's conversation partner more precise.

Of course we cannot locate a point of biological discontinuity, since this does not emerge from fossil remains, and the need for it is not universally recognized, even by those defending a theory of spirit. However, the awakening of man to his superior aspirations by a call from God is an event. Granted, we may presuppose that this openness of man to the divine has taken the form of a progressive development, an increase in his capacity for awareness. Even nowadays we can see that many people are only occasionally free beings, otherwise allowing themselves to be swayed by the pressures of the outside world (ecological or social) or by their psychological conditioning. However, it is impossible to escape the idea of a first event affirming man and establishing him as a free being, putting him in a position to exercise this freedom, in a position of choice – acceptance or rejection – when confronted with a proposal. Such an event has a personal character in that it concerns each individual, and a universal and collective character in that it concerns humanity. It is difficult to suppose that within the same space there are beings with a metaphysical vocation and others without such a vocation – a vocation, moreover, which is one of the most important characteristics of humanity.

This decisive event is not necessarily the product of a new structure. It only implies the realization of the possibilities of human freedom, since it marks a first exercising of freedom. However, it could not have been delayed very much after the realization of human aptitudes, since it is hardly probable that a God of love would have endowed beings with a capacity for a relationship with him without having revealed it to them personally. This is essentially an event of a cultural character, introducing man into a spiritual world. Man is new to his cultural domain, but puts his definitive stamp on it: for from now on it will be in this divine world that he can ground the most liberating and most promising projects on which he can build his life.

One might suppose that, since the event which sets in motion human freedom originates in a God of love who has respect for what he has made, it would take the form of the presentation of a basic choice, offered in freedom and bearing on the acceptance by humanity of a vocation to a relationship with the divine. This acceptance could correspond in some degree to a primitive covenant, destined to guide humanity towards its fulfilment, to the degree to which human beings recognize themselves as beloved creatures, responding to this vocation of love. The situation of unhappiness, hate and contradiction in which humanity finds itself shows us that man has not accepted this covenant and prefers to build up his societies without God. But God keeps coming back. One might even suppose that this situation had been foreseen by God, for ages such as our own, and that the story of original sin in Genesis is also a prophetic evocation of the tendency which man will show to banish God from his life, and the dramatic consequences which ensue.

If we adopt the perspective of a speciation by just one couple, it is easy to envisage the human species as having a single vocation, and to understand the first setback to this vocation by a single rejection of God's call as having been universal; it is equally easy to put the choice in the immediate context of the achievement of freedom by the human race; the contraction of humanity to just one couple also ensures the identity between a personal choice and a choice with universal consequences. However, this perspective hardly corresponds to the criteria of probability established by scientific arguments. On the other hand, it could emerge from the idea of a close link between the mind – or the free human spirit – and a specific mutation. The risk in such a conception is that it gives support to an inversion of the relationship between spirit and matter, representing the spirit as a consequence of matter, as a result of material evolution. Ontologically, such an inversion would seem to be impossible. However, the created spirit remains bound up with the body in a simultaneous existence, even if it is prior to it (not in time, but in initiative).

One can envisage different possibilities in connection with the creation of the individual spirit bound up with a material body. We might suppose that the creation of this spirit was additional to the evolutionary creation of the body, and came about at a point when the body was sufficiently evolved. We might also suppose that this spirit pre-existed the evolved state of the body and that it impelled the body towards the fulfilment of an evolution which opened up communication between it and the Creator. We might also suppose that the ontogenic priority of the spirit lies essentially in the Creator Spirit and that the latter creates new spirits in different ways, not excluding the slow creation resulting from a certain level of complexification of matter which would confer superior properties on the new complex.

Of course these different conceptions raise the question of the relationships (distinction and liaison) between spirit and matter; this is a problem which would call for a long discussion. Moreover, this problem has been apparent since antiquity – and without doubt before that. It arises from the intuition, in the subjective experience of human beings, of being conscious and capable of self-determination. Closely bound up with the definition of man – who discovers himself to be free in a determined world – this intuition is nevertheless condemned by certain individuals in our day on the grounds that it cannot be included within the categories of objective knowledge. However, it is hardly a real

scientific attitude to deny the existence of what one does not obtain by routes marked out *a priori*. It is alien to the scientific spirit to reject all subjective knowledge as false. The scientific spirit remains open to all possibilities in its concern for objective knowledge, and this must leave it in a position of doubt or questioning in particular circumstances where certainty might perhaps arise from another process than that of objective perception.

If we adopt the perspective of speciation by a population, the unity of vocation of the human species and the universality of the first rejection could still be based on a single population, above all if it were reduced to the dimensions of just one people. The first human societies were governed by a simple hierarchy and when the Bible, like other writings from antiquity, uses a person's name, this name often denotes a people deriving from the same ancestor or the same illustrious leader in the past. The choices in which each individual is involved thus often have a collective character bound up with the initiative of a leader of the people. In this second perspective the realization of the freedom of humanity would seem comparatively progressive and as requiring time to elapse during which the choice would be tested. That raises the question of the destiny of any human beings who might perhaps have had a capacity for freedom before the first offer of a covenant. This problem has always existed for theology, but at a different level, in the form of the redemption of people who lived before any knowledge of Christ or even before the Mosaic covenant. It calls for a response based on the essential fact of the sovereign freedom of God who is love, who pursues his design of love further than our eyes can see.

In fact God, by his very freedom, is faithful to his plan of creation and his plan of love. As for our freedom, he willed to address us by human means, by human witness; that makes the communication of his message imperfect; but the freedom of his love is not fettered by our weakness, nor trapped by our modest logic. God is capable of fulfilling all our needs, because *where it is a matter of free and conscious beings*, called to dialogue with him, he never abandons them. That might seem an evasion in the face of a lapse in logic. It is, rather, a confession of the inability of our logic to resolve all the problems which are resolved by the love of God, a natural impotence to contain this God who will not be shut up within our limits. But that does not mean that our logic is impotent to discover God.

In this perspective (but also in the previous perspective), the spirit might seem to have priority, underlying matter in a very firm bond (the separation of the spirit and the body is a 'violent' state). Drawing matter towards communication with God, the impulse of the spirit would espouse the creative process organizing this matter: it would make the material body open to this communication and thus make room for the entry of the living God into the body of creation.

Thus God penetrates his creation by a creature in his image. That does not exclude the possibility of other creatures being called to welcome God through human mediation: other creatures and indeed in one sense all creation, which St Paul tells us is groaning under the pains of giving birth (Rom. 8.19-22).

If we adopt the perspective of a speciation at the level of a number of populations, the unity of the human species remains by its genesis, implying a stage prior to a single population. The unity of the human vocation then rests on the universality of the divine call, which would be addressed to all human beings in their different places. The universality of the first rejection might seem remarkable, since it would presuppose a strange unanimity against God, and that would only be explicable on the basis of a remarkable intervention by a seductive spirit opposed to God and winning all the votes at an early stage. However, this perspective does not change anything in the conception of the spirit impelling matter towards God. It simply sheds light on the existence of another spirit, prompting rejection of God, capable of driving the efforts of the human spirit off course. It is clear that our reflections can do no more than begin to touch on questions in connection with which there is still much to discover and understand.

To sum up

We ought to keep in mind right to the end of this chapter the constant progress made from the first vertebrates to man.

Over the course of several hundred million years, the vertebrates have progressively freed themselves from their environment. In this way they have acquired increasing autonomy, which is a necessary condition for the achievement of increasingly complex behaviour. This process culminates with anatomical man. The implement which he holds in his hand is an extension of his organism, the characteristics of which he can modify at will depending on his needs and circumstances. This is no longer just a freedom from the environment, but also a conquest of this environment. The little Australopitheci with their shaped stones hunted vigorous baboons bigger than they were. Soon the projectile brought a degree of liberation from space.

Autonomy from the surrounding environment was the necessary condition for the development of a second process, the attainment of freedom. Freedom and human thought emerge together, as the being acquires a new form of autonomy, this time from the way in which he or she is determined. Acts become increasingly human the more they are dissociated from the satisfaction of an immediate need. So human behaviour comes to take on two essential characteristics:

– The realization of long-term plans (liberation from time, cf. the Neanderthal plans for the beyond).

– The possibility of choice between different plans.

It is for this form of autonomy from the self that the term freedom must be reserved.

77

Pierre Teilhard de Chardin, 1881-1955

Life

Pierre Teilhard de Chardin was born on 1 May 1881 in the family chateau of Sarcenat, near Clermont-Ferrand in France. He spent his early childhood there. Even when he was young, the volcanoes of the Le Puy chain attracted him to geology. However, on leaving school he responded to another call. In 1899 he joined the Society of Jesus. Then began a long period of literary, philosophical and theological studies which he completed in 1912; he had already been ordained to the priesthood in 1911. After that he could devote himself to science. In the autumn of 1912 he entered the laboratory of the palaeontologist Marcellin Boule who had just reported the discovery of the fossil man of Ła-Chapelle-aux-Saints. Then came the war, the whole of which he spent as a stretcher-bearer on the northern and eastern fronts. Up to that point Teilhard had lived in the closed environment of religious institutions. In the middle of tragedy, he discovered the world. It was in the trenches that he wrote down his first reflections. After being demobilized in 1919 he enrolled at the Sorbonne, obtained a degree in natural sciences and in 1922 took his doctorate in palaeontology. These were well filled years. After 1920 he taught geology and palaeontology at the Catholic Institute in Paris. His reputation was already growing in intellectual and scientific circles. His scientific activity intensified. Responding to an invitation of the Jesuit Fathers settled in China, in 1923 and 1924 he took part in two geological and palaeontological missions in the Gobi desert. It was there, in the solitude, that he composed the Mass on the World, a mystical poem which was a herald of the 'Teilhard approach'. However, it was specifically this approach, the theological repercussions of his reflections on the facts of science, that was soon to disturb an anxious hierarchy. In spring 1925 he was deprived of his chair, despite the protests of the rector of the Catholic Institute. In 1926 he set off again for China. His exile was to prove extraordinarily fertile in every way. In 1927 he finished the writing of *Le Milieu divin*, one of his major works. At the end of 1929 he was involved in the discovery of Sinanthropos, or Peking Man, the fossil man of the caves of Chou-kou-tien, near Peking. From 1930 to 1940, scientific expeditions followed one another at an increasing rate, in China, India, Java and Burma. Teilhard was invited to join in some prestigious expeditions, including the American mission to Central Asia and the Yellow Expedition made by André Citroën. He also spent some time in France and in the United States. The Second World War confined him to China. He used this time to write his best known and most significant book, *The Phenomenon of Man*. Soon after his return to France in 1946 he began to show the first symptoms of heart disease.

His position *vis-à-vis* the religious authorities did not improve, but helped by his faith and those around him he continued to have the courage to obey. In 1948 he had to refuse the chair offered him by the College of France. Although his election to the Academy of Sciences in 1950 showed how highly he was regarded by the scientific community, once again he went into exile – this time to the United States. Twice he went to South Africa, where a new adventure in human palaeontology was beginning with the discovery of the earliest fossil hominids, the Australopitheci. These new scientific facts were integrated into his writings on *Man's Place in Nature*. A last essay, 'The Christic', sums up his thought. He died on Easter Eve, 10 April 1966, in New York, at the end of an extraordinarily full life.

After his death, Teilhard's thought began to spread. His friends at last got down to publishing his works: *The Phenomenon of Man* appeared in 1955. The 1960s were marked by the publication in France and abroad of an amazing number of books, articles, theses and symposia devoted to Teilhard. In 1962 the Holy Office published a warning on his work. The centenary of his birth, celebrated in 1981, was the occasion for Cardinal Casaroli, in the name of the Pope, to pay public homage to the man and his work, in a letter addressed to the Rector of the Catholic Institute in Paris.

Times

The 'phenomenon' of Teilhard de Chardin cannot be dissociated from the history of his time. Four aspects among others ought to be stressed.

1. The first half of the twentieth century was marked by decisive progress in scientific knowledge: particle physics, biology, human palaeontology and so on. These conquests provided great scope for the reflections of speculative thinkers. There had been a good deal of progress since the time of Pascal.

2. Paradoxically, after the first triumphant accents of scientism, there came a time of disenchantment. This very period was marked by the development of philosophies of the absurd, by existentialism. Camus was to write: 'The question used to be whether life had to have a meaning in order to be lived. Here it seems, on the contrary, that it is better lived as if it has no meaning.' Humanity becomes identified with Sisyphus.

3. In the political sphere, the first decades of the twentieth century saw the affirmation of totalitarian ideologies, Marxism and Fascism, each of which claimed in its own way to present 'the new man'.

4. Faced with the upheaval of ideas, the industrial revolution, the development of the sciences, the church too often withdrew into an attitude of chilly reserve.

Humanity seemed to be being torn apart. Teilhard was aware of this and suffered as a result. His missionary vocation drove him to bear witness: 'It seems to me essential that the Christian perspectives should ultimately be presented in an organized way (a vision of the world) that fits with the modern world. How is that possible without counterbalancing the power of the Communist or Fascist solutions of the earth? . . . Too many people in the church cherish the secret hope that the nineteenth century will be wiped out and that we shall soon find ourselves in the happy times before science and revolution. For this spirit to prevail would be the final disaster, a schism with humanity.'

Thought

It has been said that Teilhard de Chardin was neither a very great philosopher nor a very good theologian. For good measure, it has been added that he was not a brilliant geologist. His real genius, his great courage, was that he exposed himself to danger by putting himself at the parting of the ways. 'Child of earth and child of heaven', as he called himself, his approach was both rational, firmly anchored in his scientific experiments, and religious, supported by the Word. In a lyrical and mystical style which might disconcert people today, his work is composed rather in the style of a polychrome engraving: on first impressions, each application of colour seems only to be part of a single project; it is only at the last inking that this reveals itself in its fullness and its coherence. A professional on the history of the earth, Teilhard puts all his reflections in a historical setting:

– Matter has a history: elementary particles, atoms, mineral molecules, organic molecules already tend towards union and complexity.

– As they continue to unite, organic molecules become parts of increasingly complex structures: that is how life has been for three and a half thousand million years.

– Palaeontology teaches us that over millions of years, life has not ceased to be organized in increasingly complex systems, which are increasingly autonomous, and increasingly endowed with consciousness: 'the substance of the cosmos has a basic tendency to organize itself and to fold in on itself.'

– Within this burgeoning of life, the 'phenomenon of man' makes its own way. The human palaeontologist retraces its course. In the course of the last millions of years, a completely new branch has emerged from the strain: animal awareness becomes the capacity to reflect, to be objective about oneself; autonomy has become freedom. With the arrival of human thought, biological evolution has somehow 'left its orbit' to escape towards the infinite. But where is it going? This means looking further. For that, it is necessary to change the scene, but Teilhard is struck by an analogy: just as matter culminates in biogenesis, so humanity transcends itself in Christogenesis, the event of Christ, Son of God, but also Son of Mary. The arrival of Christ serves to 'superanimate nature'. The incarnation is a renewal, a restoration, of all the forces and powers of the universe: the Christ is the instrument, the centre, the end of all animate and material creation. By him all things are created, sanctified and vivified. This is how the 'cosmic Christ' seemed to Teilhard.

This vision of reality gives rise to a mysticism of human action which is without doubt one of the most striking of Teilhard's contributions: 'In action, I join in the creative power of God: I coincide with it; I become not only the instrument but the living extension. . . In the name of our faith we have the right and the duty to be passionate about the things of the earth: that is where the triumph of God begins.'

Free to take control of himself (even to the point of offering his life), and free to decide his attitude towards his fellows (even to the point of dying for them), man has become this creature capable of deciding what his relation will be to his Creator.

This is the adventure of which we are told in the book of Genesis, in the words of another age.

Fr Teilhard de Chardin in 1931 during the 'Yellow Expedition'.
Photo Teilhard Foundation

5

What is Man?

If human beings are often tormented by the question of their origins and their future, it is because they discover within themselves a great need to know. It is difficult to exist, to live, to be involved in everyday struggles, desires, pleasures and suffering without an overall plan, a meaning, an end, without having any idea why, how, when and where.

So since human beings are capable of reflecting, of watching themselves live, grow and die, they are steeped in this overall and piercing question; and when they accept the question and refuse to let it be stilled, they try to give an answer.

Who are we? Where do we come from? Where are we going? Why are we alive? These are questions which we ask ourselves when we accept the minimum of solitude indispensable for the birth of real thought, disengaged from the noisy voices which seek to ensnare us, to exploit us under a thousand pretexts.

The Christian who prays and meditates on an icon of Christ and Mary knows himself or herself in a vague but confident way to be a child of God, is aware of being given existence at every moment by the Father who makes us breathe, love, live, be and grow in love. Human love for our brothers and sisters comes through a mysterious inspiration which we have learned to call the Holy Spirit, God himself.

Why do we know that? Is it because of the mysterious peace which invades our hearts and our whole beings when we collect our thoughts before the holy image? Is it this peace which

Those who keep Raising the Question of God

The question of faith

I constantly keep asking myself this question. I said no. I said no to God, putting things rather brutally, but the question constantly keeps coming back again. I keep asking myself, 'Is this possible?'

When thinking about chance, for example, I keep telling myself that it cannot be chance which combines the atoms. But if not, what? A series of questions keeps coming back, and they are always the same. I look at them again; I keep puzzling away. I am obsessed, yes, obsessed, if not by God, at least by non-God. I really am.

Jean Rostand

Those for whom the Question of God is a Matter of Taste

I believe that we must distinguish between a scientific and a non-scientific attitude. When people talk of the former, I think that they need to consider the case of practising scientists. For them the question of the existence of God does not arise. When the physicist analyses movement, force, the properties of a particle; when the biologist analyses the properties of the cell; neither their reasoning nor their hands are ever guided by the quest for a proof of the existence or non-existence of God. I think that for practising scientists this problem is utterly irrelevant. And aside from that, away from the practice of science, as far as I am concerned it is a matter of taste.

F. Jacob

gives us existential, almost experimental verification? Is it this profound intuition of our spirit which allows us to affirm that we are certain of the infinite Love which beats in our hearts?

Is it the great witness of other believers, those of our time, those of past centuries who, like us, have made a mysterious encounter through a very human sign: a face which has been illuminated, a word which has echoed without ceasing to be living and fruitful, a gesture which has helped or soothed? How do we come to be believers?

It is almost as difficult to say truly how one comes to believe in God and in his Son Jesus as it is to say why one lives, why one exists. Some people suddenly find themselves believers after years of talking in a familiar way with the One to whom their parents introduced them as the Father of heaven. Others follow a different course; there was a time before their conversion and there is a time after it; they often speak of the birth of their faith with passion and emotion; sometimes they, too, cannot say when light dawned on them, when the spring began to flow.

However, almost all of us share a particular point of reference with other believers and especially with the founders of our community of faith, those who were sent by Jesus of Nazareth, who, though he was dead, was yet proclaimed as the Living One (Acts 25.19).

One can be a Christian and feel oneself in deep, though not total communion, with other men and women, people with other beliefs. We are preoccupied with the same basic questions; our replies agree on certain points regarding man, history and society; on other more metaphysical or symbolic levels they diverge. Thus dialogues, confrontations, even polemic goes on over the centuries between Christians and members of other religions, believers in God and unbelievers, agnostics and atheists.

A Form of Neo-Atheism

I do not reject the question (of God), but it is not my problem. Let us say that I do not ask myself whether or not there is a God because it is clear that I do not believe in God or in what goes to make up the concept of God. That is so in the case both of the God of the religious and the God of the philosophers. In this sense I can call myself an atheist, but having done that I immediately feel the need to say more precisely what I am, in terms – shall we say – of a neo-atheism.

Neo-atheism takes account of the fact that religion is to be found not only in what is called religion, but everywhere. Reason, with a capital R, is a religion; ideas can take the place of God; magic lends support to what we believe to be an empirical view of things. That having been said, I am clear that I find it absolutely impossible to believe in revealed deities. That is the first aspect of my neo-atheism.

The second aspect is that there is an unexplained and inexplicable dimension. When I hear talk of a negative theology, of the other side of the coin, of something that has not yet found a name, I know that it is important for me. One can explain everything except one essential dimension in everything. I have a profound sense of 'mystery'.

Edgar Morin

If the time of mutual mistrust is past or almost past, a good deal of courage and humility is needed to listen in truth and to share the way. To do that calls for honesty and disinterestedness which can cost a very great deal. Is that why we increasingly find ourselves listening to speeches which are insensitive statements rather than communications, discussions which, whether explicitly or not, are aimed more at reassuring supporters bolstering up institutions than at bearing witness to aspects of the truth which we have been allowed to discover?

These reflections bring us to the aim of this second part of our reflection. We are not out to convince at any price – i.e. at the price of excessive simplification or partisan caricature – those who do not believe in God the Creator and Saviour. We respect their freedom too much for that, and our God even more! We are not in the business of providing cheap reassurance for Christians by means of intellectual sleight of hand, skilfully avoiding questions by not answering them or pretending not to feel real difficulties, dismissing them as clumsiness or failure to adapt to the official language of the Catholic Church. We combine this attitude, which is inspired by a concern for intellectual rigour, with a deep attachment to our own church.

Our aim is to give an answer, in faith, to the question 'What is man?' We are particularly concerned to reply to some of the questions which come more naturally to believers familiar with the language of scripture, who also have some knowledge of the main discoveries of cosmology, biology and palaeontology over the last fifty years.

Our plan would be hopelessly ambitious if we tried to be encyclopaedic. That is in no way our intention. We hope to provide an account which is mainly concerned with the quest for meaning and coherence, open to new developments, a modest but serious contribution to this passionate discovery of the genesis of humanity.

Reading Genesis

When the Christian believer thinks of creation, a variety of expressions will spontaneously come to mind.

They may be those of the early creed:

I believe in God, the Father Almighty,
Maker of heaven and earth.

They may be those of the psalms which we sometimes read or sing:

Our help is in the name of the Lord
who made heaven and earth (Ps. 124.8).

The whole of Psalm 104 is a hymn to the splendours of creation:

Bless the Lord, O my soul!
O Lord my God, thou art very great!
Thou hast stretched out the heavens like a
tent,
and hast laid the beams of thy chambers on the
waters (Ps. 104.1, 2–3).

Psalm 136, the great liturgy which the Jews call the Great Hallel, is even more lyrical:

O give thanks to the Lord, for he is good,
for his steadfast love endures for ever . . .
to him who alone does great wonders,
for his steadfast love endures for ever;
to him who by understanding made the
heavens . . .
to him who spread out the earth upon the
waters (Ps. 136.1-6).

Praise and adoration are mingled in these cries of jubilation, in which the believer never separates the work of salvation, the liberation of Israel and its creation as a people, from the primordial work, the making of the heavens, establishment of the dry land on the waters, and so on.

These psalms follow the order of cosmogony in the first chapter of Genesis. What is surprising about that?

The sages and thinkers of Israel had long meditated on the beginning of the human adventure, as on other great stages in the life of Israel.

After the exile, when some wise men personified Wisdom and claimed that she had been created before even the earliest work of God, other scribes, reviving old oral traditions and old documents, elaborated the first three chapters of Genesis by bringing together two currents, the earlier one called Yahwistic and the later one called Priestly.

These two narratives seek to reply on the one hand to pagan cosmogonies and theogonies which gave other interpretations of the origins of humanity, and on the other hand to questions which Israelite believers, heirs of the traditions of the patriarchs, the Exodus and the kingdom, still continued to raise.

Here they were, living on the basis of a covenant between God and their people, in the midst of persecution, experiencing evil, suffering and death, constantly threatened by unfaithfulness and idolatry. What was the origin of earth and heaven? Who had made the sun and the moon that the other religions had divinized? Why man and animals? Why the human couple and its fertility? Why the experience of evil and the wrath of God? Why suffering and death?

These were vital questions to which answers had to be given if believers were to be clear about their relationship with Yahweh, the world, his history and other peoples. There was a basic need of meaning and understanding which could only be satisfied in a theology which integrated myths and symbols in a coherent way with the experience of the covenant between the God of Abraham, Isaac and Jacob and his people.

Looking for the beginning

In an excellent short book entitled *Believing in Original Sin Today*, Pierre Gibert offers some brief thoughts on the question of beginnings. Even in everyday life it is almost impossible to find a beginning: we cannot personally grasp the moment of our birth nor the moment of the birth of our people. We always have to resort to other witnesses. Even to be able to ask about our birth presupposes not only that we have been born but above all that we have lived long enough to be able to reflect rationally and with awareness on our personal origins. That presupposes that we can find witnesses who have retained memories which by definition are not accessible to us.

It is out of the question to expect direct knowledge of the beginning of humanity or the universe. Christian faith may affirm that God and the angels, good and bad, were there, but they are hardly historical witnesses in the usual sense of the term. A history of the origin of humanity as told by witnesses is, and always will be, impossible.

On the other hand, as Pierre Gibert points out, it is possible to hazard a guess on another level, by reflecting on actual experience: the Bible and the people of Israel bear witness to that reflection and that experience in the first chapters of Genesis.

At the time when the final version of these chapters was written, round about the fifth and sixth centuries BC, Israel had already had experience on the one hand of having been saved and created as people of God, and on the other of sin and evil.

'The people whom I formed for myself that they might declare my praise' (Isa. 43.21). Israel is a people created by God. This people knows itself to be chosen, as Deuteronomy constantly says. 'For you are holy to the Lord your God; the Lord your God has chosen you to be a people for his own possession, out of all the peoples that are upon the face of the earth' (Deut. 7.6).

'Correlatively,' continues Pierre Gibert, 'for Israel, to be created means to be saved. Israel was saved from Pharaoh, from Egypt and the Red Sea and the desert – all dangers representing evil. And it was the fact of having escaped these dangers which equally allowed it to become a people, the people of God.'

This double experience of creation and salvation necessarily affected the Israelite conception of the creation of the world; and in fact in Gen. 1 the world emerges from a separation of the waters (Gen. 1.6-10), just as Israel had passed through the waters of the Red Sea, which were split in two, and appeared on the dry land of the Sinai desert.

We can see how this twofold experience would underlie all the reflections of the wise men of Israel on the beginning of their people.

In a later chapter we shall be discussing the experience of sin and evil and the quest for its origins.

Genesis 1-3: The problem of myth: Adam and the original couple

Many ways of reading Genesis are suggested today:

– Naive and historicizing readings, which provoke polemic or violent rejection on the part of those nowadays whose minds have been shaped by the progress of science.

– More knowledgable readings revolve around the question of myth. Does the Bible use mythical language? But in that case, what is the difference between this language and the pagan myths of Babylon and Sumeria?

Some people stress that the wise men of Israel practised demythologizing, but continue to be disturbed by certain stories with particular images: the Garden of Eden, the story of the giants in Gen. 6, and so on.

To clarify the discussion a little, it may be useful to define more closely two possible meanings of the word myth.

1. First of all, myth can be understood as being, 'A narrative construction which projects on to "primordial time" a certain archetype of earthly realities and human action in the form of a model story about the life of the gods' (P. Grelot).

Thus the story of the creation of the world, in the Babylonian poem, projects us into the primordial time of the gods. The account of what the gods do and say is a kind of explanation of the appearance of humanity and allows us to identify a number of distinctive human features.

Fundamentalism

This term suggests a return to the sources, attachment to the foundations of a faith or a commitment. And in fact fundamentalist attitudes have often been lived out with a sense of unshakable fidelity. People are fundamentalist in a confession when they feel rigorously bound by the letter of the initial prescriptions of its founder. In connection with reading the Bible, fundamentalism denotes the attitude which attributes a literal meaning to the biblical texts (at least in translation), refusing the shifts in meaning which others accept by referring to cultural changes which have come about since the redaction of the biblical texts. This attitude is in no way a rejection of the profound meaning of the biblical texts; however, these texts are accepted, in both form and content, as total truth coming to God as they stand.

To tell the truth, no one ever puts this attitude into practice completely. In the Bible there are always texts which are clearly narrative rather than exemplary. It can even be noted that at all times the biblical texts have always been more or less interpreted by the religious and inspired minds which have used them (cf. Paul's Letter to the Galatians on the subject of Sarah and Hagar).

Be this as it may, a relatively fundamentalist attitude has long been prevalent in the reading of the Bible, giving numerous terms their literal meaning without excluding their message of revelation. This attitude has had the merit of preserving faithfully the form of this message at times when there was a danger that repetition from memory, or later re-copying, might distort it.

However, as human civilization has been transformed by the acquisition of more precise knowledge about the universe, the earth and the living world, fundamentalist attitudes have come up against serious obstacles. The Galileo affair is a model instance here: the church authorities did not accept that the earth revolved round the sun, since the Bible was produced in a cultural context in which the sun was thought to revolve round the earth; it was not the earth but the sun which Joshua had stopped in order to win the battle completely.

When exegesis developed, it set about showing that biblical terms used the language of a particular period and civilization to convey a message of eternal revelation; the words and concepts in the language used were not in themselves eternal. So a good deal of caution and awareness was needed to discern the authentic message revealed in its linguistic and cultural vehicle. This recognition also had important implications for the message itself. For what the inspired author has a mission to announce is not the cultural context of his time; on the contrary, the essential feature of his message often lies in what makes his words original over against this cultural context; the form of the language is just a way chosen to express the message. Thus modern biologists are well aware that grain sown in the ground does not die. But that does not in any way reduce the significance of the biblical image of the grain which 'dies' in order to bear fruit. We know that this imagery signifies Christ, dead and put in the tomb (sown in the earth) to inaugurate the resurrection. We know that the imagery used here is meant to convey that the grain loses its identity as grain that can be used for food (it was thought to die when it germinated), in order to transform itself when sown in the ground, the food reserves which constitute the grain disappearing for the benefit of a new growth. Of course, no one would think of defending the view that grain dies and revives.

The scientific discoveries of our time sometimes radically put in question the cultural patterns of the biblical period. Not only is the way of life of the majority of Westerners no longer either nomadic or pastoral, but the reality of the world is increasingly illuminated by scientific facts: these make our knowledge more accurate, explain mechanisms, produce models which are very different from the necessarily restricted and simplified views of a non-scientific era, particularly in connection with creation and the origin of man. The fundamentalist attitude becomes very difficult, since it has to reject the increasingly categorical affirmations of science in order to preserve a faith unreservedly bound to numerous cultural details of the period when it was proclaimed. Certainly, faith is a very precious matter: but we have to make room for a proper exegesis and the indubitable contributions made by science (which is knowledge received from the creator) in order to be able to recognize better the essential message or revelation and to welcome it in a serene and outgoing faith. The only way out of situations which have been blocked in this way lies in the quest for the profound demands of God which lie beyond the form of the messages we have received.

For example, if a man feels the forces of evil within himself, it is because in his blood he has the blood of a fallen god Kingu, the chief of the rebel gods.

If a man feels that he is the plaything of cosmic powers, it is because the god Ea has enrolled him in the service of the gods.

We can see that the Yahwistic and Priestly stories are already a long way from these pagan conceptions. Besides, such conceptions were violently rejected by the first Christian thinkers, who described them with scorn as *mythoi* (fables or legends).

2. However, the word myth has a second sense. This other conception, which we would call more philosophical or more theological, sees it as 'the effort made by the human imagination to give concrete representation to certain realities which essentially escape the experience of the senses but nevertheless have a place in religious experience'.

Here mythical awareness is contrasted with historical awareness. The historian tries to reconstruct sequences of facts as exactly as possible by interrogating witnesses and giving as objective an interpretation as possible of their evidence. There will be little scope for the imagination, and it will be strictly controlled by the evidence.

Mythical awareness does not appeal to any historical evidence. On the contrary, it proves its creativity by creating images and symbols, also presented in narrative form, intended to explain certain major facts of religious experience. The aim of this narrative will be to reply to important questions posed by humanity. In the imagery it uses it will frequently resort to simple analogies drawn from historic human experience.

In this second sense, the word myth can be used in connection with the narratives in Gen. 1-3.

Here we certainly have a narrative stemming from the creative imagination of inspired authors replying on pre-existent material: polytheistic myths, great symbols like the tree of life, the serpent, the Garden of Eden, and so on.

The Organization of the Universe in Egypt

Shu, the god of the air, separates Nut, his daughter, the heavenly vault, from Geb, his son, the earth (Egyptian papyrus from between 1100 and 950 BC).

A hymn, written about 1400 BC, celebrates the sun god Amon, who goes through the night to rise upon sleeping humanity. He is father of all the gods, and they sing his praises:

They say to you, 'Welcome, father of the fathers of all the gods,
who raised the heaven and laid out the earth,
who made what is and created what will be,
we offer hymns to you because you have wearied yourself with us.'

(from *Near Eastern Religious Texts relating to the Old Testament*, SCM Press and Westminster Press 1978, p.15)

The narrative is also based on the simplest religious and human experience: the nearness of God, the experience of sin and guilt, the experience of sexual desire, of intercourse, of nudity and of shame. It uses anthropomorphisms which only disturb the theological purists: God walking in the garden in the evening.

The controlling factor of the narrative is the certainty of the existence of one God who made a covenant with his people and who created heaven and earth. Many beings and gods who populated ancient imagination disappeared in the world as imagined by the wise men of Israel: the sun and the moon are no longer gods. The one God is he who is invisible and who revealed his name in the burning bush (Ex. 3).

Thus the narrative of Gen. 1-3 is a theological and anthropological synthesis. In a mythical style it presents an original monotheistic construction, which takes account of the experience

Egyptian Hymn to the Sun God Aten

Here are some extracts from this hymn, composed by Pharaoh Akhenaten.

You shine out in beauty on the horizon of heaven,
O living disc, the beginning of life.
When you have appeared on the eastern horizon,
you have filled every land with your perfection.
When you set on the western horizon,
the earth lies in darkness as in death.
The earth lies in silence,
for the one who created it has gone to rest on his horizon.
Then the earth becomes bright: you have arisen on the horizon.
As solar disc, you shine by day.
Men awaken and stand on their feet.
Their arms are bent in worship, because you appear.
The whole land goes to work.
All beasts are satisfied with their pasture,
the trees and plants become green.
The birds flutter in their nests,
raising their wings in worship before your spirit.
The ships sail upstream and down.
The fish in the river dart before your face.
You make the seed grow in women,
make fluid into mankind.
How manifold are your works!
They are hidden from the face of man,
O sole God, apart from whom there is no other.
You have made people for yourself,
the Lord of all of them,
wearying himself with them,
the Lord of the whole land, rising for them.
You are in my heart. . .

(*Near Eastern Religious Texts*, pp.16ff.).

The Organization of the Universe in Babylon

The poem Enuma Elish tells of the birth of the gods through Apsu, the male principle, and Tiamat, the female principle. Tiamat wants to destroy the young gods, who are disturbing her. They delegate their power to Marduk (the god of Babylon). He kills Tiamat and the gods allied with her. Then he forms the world from her body.

Marduk strengthened his hold on the vanquished gods,
and turned back to Tiamat whom he had bound.
With his unsparing mace he crushed her skull,
then the lord rested and contemplated her corpse,
intent on dividing the form and doing skilful works.
He split it like a dried fish,
set up one half and made it the firmament,
drew a skin over it, posted guards
and instructed them not to let its water escape.

(*Near Eastern Religious Texts*, p.83)

One might compare this myth with the story in Gen. 1 and also with a different myth often represented in Egyptian sculpture.

of the covenant and the spiritual freedom of human beings. Its specific aim is to explain the origins of this experience: a free initiative of God, who wants to communicate his own inner richness – 'Let us make man in our image and our likeness' – and who requires of men and women filial obedience if they seek to obtain immortality.

If we accept this way of understanding the language of Genesis, the literary genre of which recalls both the Wisdom literature and the style of myth, we have considerable freedom in interpreting the story of the creation of man and the original couple.

It is now clear that this story does not claim to give us any information of a palaeontological kind relating to the different possible theories of the origin of man: whether humanity derives from just one couple, one population, or several populations. These notions are totally unknown to the authors of Genesis. By introducing Adam and then his wife Eve, they simply want to indicate the profound union existing between man and woman (taken from man's side, 'bone of my bone, flesh of my flesh').

On the other hand, the image of descent from just one couple is a very suitable symbol for the unity of the human race, which is both a fact of experience and a christological certainty. That does not mean, however, that scripture tells us plainly as revealed truth that God could only have created humanity from just one couple. Granted, the Roman Catholic Church thought that it could affirm this down to *Humani Generis* (1950), which was endorsed by Paul VI in 1963. However, we think that this scruple is no longer necessary, and we subscribe to the opinion of Fr Grelot, who wrote in 1973:

'As for exegesis, it states that revelation strongly affirms human unity, taking up the history of our race at the level of our shattered unity. But it sheds no direct light on the way in which this unity was originally achieved, whether as biological unity based on a single "mutant" couple (monogenism) or social unity based on a group of mutants already forming a society (polygenism), or on a convergent unity resulting from the regrouping of several groups of mutants (polyphyletism).

The essential thing is not to choose *a priori* between these forms, all of which are theoretically possible from a scientific point of view, but to note that all must result in the living awareness of a unity which is both necessary (because it constitutes the human race) and impossible (because it is contradicted by the establishment of the race and its sinful condition). Moreover, in the present state of our knowledge, palaeontology cannot yet say precisely at what level of the development we should locate hominization in

The Birth of Eve, 1478 engraving, Bibliothèteque Alibaux, Lyons

the strict sense, i.e. the existence of a "self-awareness" which carries with it the possibility of a moral and spiritual experience, however primitive one that might be supposed to be.

So it would be wise not to aim at a new "concordat" between science and religion, although it would be useful to understand how anthropological enquiries can be reconciled with the demands of faith.'

The famous dispute over the relative merits of polygenism or monogenism can be abandoned if we adopt the epistomological viewpoint briefly expounded at the beginning of this chapter.

So we are rid of an intellectual conflict from which our parents suffered. We can now re-read these texts in peace, and be free to enjoy their extraordinary poetic and spiritual atmosphere. Who can ever tire of the riches of the imagery employed here, in particular the picture of 'man formed out of the dust of the earth' into whose 'nostrils God breathes the breath of life'? (Gen. 2.7). Does not this simple verse alone call us to prayer and thanksgiving?

Creation

Most holy Father,
we proclaim your greatness.
You have created all things with wisdom and love.
You have made human beings in your image
and you have entrusted the universe to them,
that as servants to you, their Creator,
they might reign over creation.

Creation. That is what we like to call all of reality that springs from the will of God, what we are and what surrounds us. Creation: this term does not evoke so much the very first moment of time or an initial setting in motion; if it denotes a remote origin in time, it signifies rather the actual bond between the Invisible One and all of existence that goes to make up the world in its reality and its dynamism. The creature exists, in true independence; it is not God, nor is it a part of the divine. But it does not exist like a child abandoned by a parent. 'He himself gives to all men life and breath and everything. . . Yet he is not far from each one of us, for "In him we live and move and have our being"' (Acts 17.25-28).

The Bishops of France

6

The Experience of Evil and Sin and the Quest for Origins

A shelter in Paris during the early days of the Second World War. *Photo Viollet*

Among the questions which beset our age, that of evil in all its forms is perhaps the most painful and sometimes even the most obsessive. Some things are understandable. We may analyse easily enough the political and economic causes of certain wars. We may even have an explanation for certain social scourges (road accidents, lung cancer among smokers, deaths from alcoholism or drugs). There human responsibility is direct and often personal. Patient social education can remedy it. . . But what about those insidious diseases which defy the progress of medical science, however amazing: the excessive suffering of so many innocent victims, children foremost among them; the nightmare of serious mental illnesses, some of which are hereditary; the great natural scourges (earthquakes, tidal waves, droughts, floods) which are too devastating for modern technology to alleviate? All these violent occurrences, so hostile to humanity and to life in all its animal and plant forms, raise some formidable questions.

Why? Why does it happen? What can human beings do? Why does God let it happen? Is there a hidden source of evil in the world? Has evil been in existence since man? Before man? From the beginning of the universe, at that zero point of space and time which were then impelled outwards with the colossal energy of the big bang?

Do counter-energy, counter-information, dis-information introduce aberrant parameters into the course of the thousands of millions of years of cosmic, galactic and then terrestrial revolution?

This is a formidable question, since palaeontology shows us the cruelty of animal habits before man, the wretched conditions in which the first anthropoids lived, the stammering responses to the deaths of our first ancestors, which was perhaps still like that of animals, several hundred millions of years ago.

The question is a formidable one, since civilized man has always had to live in fear: of his fellow human beings; of his physical death; of dangerous invisible forces: hostile deities, demons, evil spirits, sorcerers, and so on.

The question is obscurely bound up with and clouded by the way in which human beings have felt their relationship with the divine to be marred; they have often had a sense of being alienated, crushed, sometimes terrified by the will, not to mention the caprice, which they attributed to God or the gods.

Sometimes, in proud revolt against the deity, human beings have gone so far as to claim all his prerogatives, even denying his very existence. This has especially been the case in the West since the nineteenth century.

Physical and spiritual evil are seen as one by those who are overwhelmed by both its aspects: need, suffering, absence, solitude, collapse, intellectual and spiritual blindness.

In that case should we first seek to soothe, or rather to understand and explain? Should we look for a root? Or a beginning in time? Or a radical metaphysical or chronological origin?

It is intolerable to suffer without reason; that generates an oppressive and suicidal anxiety. In such a situation men and women need an explanation in order to attack the evil and provide themselves with a better defence. They will even create imaginary monsters symbolizing their adversary in order to fend it off better and free themselves from it.

Demonologies abound in all the pagan religions, and monsters abound in ancient imagination. Today these diabolical areas of the unfettered imagination find expression in art and especially in the cinema, into which the caverns of the collective infernal unconscious publicly pour out their contents.

One cannot hold back these black horses indefinitely; they have to be allowed some freedom to gallop, on pain of breaking down the temples and other edifices of our everyday rational awareness.

The human quest has lasted for hundreds of thousand of years. The religions of world civili-

---

Those who are Scandalized by Evil

I must say that I am extremely troubled because I cannot accept the faith of my childhood, and in particular the thought expressed by Christ, which I believe to be as false as it is beautiful, that God is Love. If I accept that there is a universe, that an omnipotent and omniscient God governs it, that is hardly love! Observing the world forces me to conclude that the life of beings is based on the death of beings, from the top of the scale to the bottom.

Alfred Kastler

zations, perhaps to be dated over the last ten thousand years, have produced responses which are at the same time complex, subtle and often wrong on important points.

'Do not believe these *mythoi*, fables,' said the fathers of the church in the first centuries after Christ. They wanted to rid their audience of many popular and harmful ideas.

An uninitiated modern reader runs the risk of being deceived by the rudimentary responses that he or she will find in the Old Testament. Its cultural context is too far from our own. Numerous conversations with scientists and modern young people have convinced us of this.

That is why we shall not begin our search for a reply to the question which torments us by looking at the Yahwistic narrative in Genesis, produced in the sixth century BC from an earlier account. We shall first look for illumination in the New Testament, persuaded that the light of Christ has priority for us. It is deeper, more all-embracing, and nearer to our culture and the history of our thought and science.

The light of the new covenant

What happened on the evening of the famous first day of the week, our first Sunday, was that the risen Christ appeared to his apostles, who were still suffering under the blow they had experienced as a result of the terrible drama which had befallen them: the unjust trial, torture and death of the one they believed to be the Messiah, the one who was to have re-established the kingdom.

Victorious over his adversaries, over lies, hate, suffering and even death, Christ appeared to his disciples saying, 'Peace be with you' (John 20.19).

The adversary

In doing this, Christ triumphed over his worst adversary, the one who manipulated the Pharisees through their wounded pride and Pilate through his weakness, the one whom Jesus himself called the devil.

Jesus clearly unmasked his adversary in terms which owe nothing to ancient imagery: 'He was a murderer from the beginning, and has nothing to do with the truth, because there is no truth in him. When he lies, he speaks according to his own nature, for he is a liar and the father of lies' (John 8.44).

What interests us most is that the one who is the word of God made flesh, the light of the world, the way, the truth, tells us that his adversary is a liar, and that from the beginning, as part of the very principle of the world, he is a murderer.

This reveals a vital truth to us:

Evil is not simply an absence, a lack, disorder, a recent or even ancient confusion. From the beginning, from the very creation of man – the Greek text here uses the same expression that we find in Matt. 19.4 as a reference to the creation of man by God and ultimately to the very origin of the world (Gen. 2.24; Gen. 1.1) – from this beginning there has been the father of lies who is nevertheless a creature subject in a certain way to the decisions of God. The light that is shed is more intense than the simple belief of the narrator of Genesis, who merely speaks of the tempter, disguised in the form of the serpent (Gen. 3.1), 'more subtle than any other wild creature', which persuaded the woman to disobey God. However, the action is the same, since it is the lie which leads to the break between man and God.

Similarly, the blinded Pharisees declare that Jesus is possessed and a Samaritan (John 8.48).

The problem with the imagery of the serpent is that it makes our contemporaries smile. They think that it is a naive image which simply represents a purely human experience. They themselves innocently suppose that they are no longer threatened these days by the tempter, who again leads them into error by persuading them that the devil no longer exists. The trick is to make people believe that this is a simple way of speaking of human freedom and the battles which must be fought against the enemy within. Here we have a new version of the scene of the temptation and the fall.

The best way of avoiding it is to take seriously this saying of Jesus in John 8.44.

So this verse has shown us something important, and we shall see that it sends us back to the whole history of man with God, and particularly to its beginnings.

Man and woman

Another episode in the New Testament will give us further light from a different direction. When asked about divorce by the Pharisees, Jesus replied:

'Have you not read that he who made them from the beginning made them male and female, and said, "For this reason a man shall leave his father and mother and be joined to his wife, and the two shall become one"? So they are no longer two but one. What therefore God has joined together, let no man put asunder' (Matt. 19.4-6).

Jesus comes to restore the first dignity of marriage spoilt by the hardness of human hearts. For *in the beginning* there was neither hardness of hearts, nor repudiation, nor divorce between man and woman, nor divorce between man and God. At this very beginning, when man and woman truly came from the hands of God, when they emerged from evolution as God wanted them, there could be no estrangement between them, no breakdown in communication, no mistrust or repudiation, any more than there could be fear of God or shame. Jesus' saying, like another that we shall be studying, sends us back to the roots of the creative act and prepares us to reflect on the depth and the theological relevance of the two narratives in Genesis. Both of them shed light on the origin of humanity, one on our freedom and one on the spiritual evil which is to have incalculable consequences, the worst of which is human death.

Jesus confronted with human death

When Jesus arrives at the tomb of his friend Lazarus, he tells us something of the secret of his life. He announces the resurrection of Lazarus, but above all he announces that he himself is the resurrection.

'I am the resurrection and the life; he who believes in me, though he die, yet shall he live, and whoever lives and believes in me shall never die' (John 11.25).

Now it is in rising from the dead that Jesus attests the truth of this saying. Or rather, by raising his Son from the dead, the Father accredits him in our eyes. Thus, by dying for us, Jesus is victor over death. It is not that he relieves us of the painful experience of seeing our strength decline and feeling that we are wrenched out of our bodies, but that he gives us the certainty that we shall meet God again when we leave our earthly life and that we shall rediscover a spiritual and bodily wholeness beyond anything that we can hope for and imagine.

The important thing, in the face of this fact and this hope, is to remind ourselves of the question with which we began. Why evil? Why this dramatic experience of human death? Why are we subjected to such a plunge into nothingness? Who is responsible for a situation so desperate that only the Son of God can deliver us from it?

Paul's reflections in Romans lead us to discover that sin separates man from God. This separation is death: spiritual and eternal death, of which physical death is the sign (cf. Wisdom 2.24; Heb. 6.1).

We all know his famous remark, which lends itself to so many interpretations:

'Therefore as sin came into the world through one man and death through sin, and so death spread to all men because all men sinned. . .' (Rom. 5.12).

This light, coming as much from Jesus himself as from Paul's reflections, sends us back to the origin of physical and spiritual death, and of its bond with sin experienced as divorce from God.

To sum up, three sayings of Christ, on three aspects of evil – the Devil, divorce between man and woman, and death – have sent us back to the beginning. So we shall now analyse the famous account of the fall of our first parents, as it was understood by the thinkers of the old covenant.

The test of freedom and the drama of the cross

We shall opt for discussing the second creation story, the one known as the 'Yahwistic narrative'. That is the only one to contain the basic episode of the temptation in Paradise, human disobedience and the banishment from the garden of Eden. We shall keep to Genesis 3, recalling that its final version dates from round about the time of the fall of the monarchy of Judah in the sixth century BC. This Yahwistic tradition, which contains many earlier features, some of which go back to the time of the patriarchs, is characterized by a naive and concrete style. The narrator does not hesitate to speak of God in very vivid terms. 'They heard the voice of the Lord God walking in the garden in the cool of the day' (Gen. 3.8).

If we are to understand the doctrinal consequences of the choices with which our first ancestors were presented, we must realize that the experience of Israel, shaped by the Exodus from Egypt and the long journey through the desert, was structured on a simple choice: happiness or unhappiness, life or death, fidelity or infidelity to the covenant.

'See, I have set before you this day life and good, death and evil' (Deut. 30.15).

'You shall live . . . if you do not hear, you shall perish' (Deut. 30.18).

Israel experienced this dramatic choice down the centuries after Abraham, through Moses, and then through the first kings. Saul symbolizes the mortal choice, and David the choice for God, despite a grave sin which brought down on him exemplary punishment (II Sam. 12-18).

It is this experience of the covenant, and of choice, which makes up the test with which human beings are confronted, involving them in a struggle for or against God, that we find projected back on the first beginnings in the story of the fall of Adam and Eve.

This story illuminates the sinful condition of man in the light of the experience of the covenant and the historical choice which Israel continued to remember, but it cannot in any way be a faithful description of the manner of this fall. Only the consequences of the fall are known. If we accept whole-heartedly this way of reading the story, we dissociate ourselves from the ancient theory of the *peccatum originans*, i.e. the first sin, which is supposed to be the cause of *peccatum originatum*, i.e. original sin. This ancient portrayal of the first sin, excessively historicized, continues to weigh on the imagination of Christians, especially on those whom a desire for security tempts to return to a literal, even fundamentalist, reading of Genesis.

Freed from this temptation to want to know too much from its anecdotal forms, we can accept and admire this fine narrative, which gives us a basically optimistic view of God and man.

Again closely following the analysis by Fr Grelot, we may note the wealth of symbols which appear in the narrative.

The tree of the knowledge of good and evil symbolizes the limits which God has put on human choice, and the obedience which is required of us. Man, to whom the universe has been entrusted, and to whom a helpmeet and a companion has been given, is not the absolute master of his future. God is not envious of him, but asks him to be receptive to him and not to want to take his place. Consequently man cannot be the master of the knowledge of good and evil, and ultimately be the equal of God.

Now man is set in a world in which there is already an intelligent force of evil which introduces suspicion. Symbolized by the serpent, the one whom Jesus called the father of lies and a murderer from the beginning, it insinuates doubt into the woman's mind: if God forbade them this tree, it was to disguise his fear of seeing man become a god with the knowledge of good and evil.

The lie seduces the woman (the symbol of the frailty in human beings) and the couple's union and mutual trust turn against the intentions of the Creator, leading to their rebellion. The lure of a superhuman knowledge, giving exceptional clairvoyance, is one of the most violent and subtle human temptations. We have seen that it can even find its way into theological discussion. Theologians who claim to know more than they really do can open the way to the persecution of courageous voices which call for more modesty. The church's past bears witness to this.

More insidious, however, are the forms of gnosis, syncretism, pseudo-sciences, theories which seek to be above all religion, above all divine revelation, 'above good and evil', to quote a famous phrase. They reproduce the old temptation which, from Solomon to Saul, from Aaron to Lot's wife, from Abraham's pagan ancestors to the very first human beings endowed with the faculties of understanding and choice, embody the refusal of the loving filial obedience of which only Jesus and Mary give us the perfect examples.

The consequences of estrangement

Don't let's fool ourselves. It is not because we said that we do not know how this divorce came about, the result of man's bad choice, that we do not think that there was really a divorce and tragic estrangement between God and the millions of people who lived before Abraham. The

Sculptures of the story of Adam and Eve on the porch of the loggia of La Saint-Chappelle in Paris
Photo Viollet

God shows Adam the tree of the knowledge of good and evil

Adam and Eve eat the fruit of the tree

analogy between the murderous folly of our age at the end of the second millennium AD, like that of previous ages, and the murder of Abel by Cain, is so striking that we hardly need to dwell on it. However far our historical awareness goes back in time, it finds itself confronted with inner jealousy, the desire to kill fellow human beings, and an inability for real love. But what we know from the secret longings of our hearts and what we hear from the mouth of the prophets is that we are called to 'love our neighbour as ourselves' (Lev. 19.28).

This hate among fellow human beings, like the lack of harmony between couples, and like the difficulties with nature experienced in work, follows from the estrangement from God experienced in every age, which also emerged in the distant past, at the time of the first beginnings of humanity. In this perspective we find that the traditional idea of original sin is dissociated from excessively naive representations and better integrated into the universal sinfulness of humanity.

Adam and Eve driven out of earthly paradise by the angel

God gives Adam and Eve a tool and clothing, symbols of their new form of existence

That is the significance of the main divine statements about the punishment of woman and the punishment of man. We may conclude the discussion with the main cause of human anguish. 'You are dust, and to dust you shall return' (Gen. 3.16).

Is human death a punishment?

It is clear that down the centuries Christians have understood death as they have experienced it, in anguish and solitude, with the temptation of doubt and the fear of dissolution into nothingness, to be the consequence of original sin. Adam and Eve were the chief culprits. Without their disobedience man would have been immortal, established for ever in original justice. That is a simplified version of what has usually been taught.

For about fifty years generally, and for the past ten years more officially in Catholic circles, a distinction has been made between physical death as a biological phenomenon and the existential and spiritual experience of death. An increasing number of Christian thinkers have considered physical death, i.e. the cessation of vital functions and then the disappearance of the corpse, as a natural phenomenon, intrinsic to life and even indispensable to the evolution of the species. The universality of the phenomenon allows it to be integrated into the very process of creation and prevents its being understood as an unfortunate accident, the simple consequence of an unprogrammed misunderstanding between God and his creature.

A well-known theologian, G. Martelet, has commented on this quite bluntly: 'Bound up with the finite universe which shapes us and leaves its stamp on us, death, our death, terrible though it may be, would seem to be not so much a punishment as the cosmic sign of our finitude.'

This idea is familiar to scientists, but perhaps less so to Christians with a traditional background.

What is the problem with this? It is that the Bible always talks of death not as a phenomenon natural to every living species but as a drama

Extract from a Profession of Faith by Paul VI

We believe that in Adam all have sinned. This signifies that the original sin committed by him made human nature fall. This fall is common to all men and women, so that they now bear the consequences of this fault. Thus their state is not that of our first parents, created in holiness and justice, and knowing neither evil nor death. It is human nature thus fallen, stripped of the grace in which it was clothed, sapped of its own natural strength, and subject to the empire of death, that is transmitted to all men; and it is in this sense that every man is born in sin.

So we believe, with the Council of Trent, that original sin is transmitted with human nature, 'not by imitation but by propagation', and that in this way it is universal.

We believe that Our Lord Jesus Christ, by the sacrifice of the cross, has redeemed us from original sin and all the personal sins committed by each of us, so that, according to the word of the apostle, 'where sin abounded, grace abounded even more'.

experienced by sinful man. Now it is said of that kind of death, 'God did not make death' (Wisdom 1.13a).

It is from this tragic death, as from the agony of Job, that Christ has come to free us by living it out in a way that we could hardly expect, even to the point of being abandoned on the cross: 'My God, my God, why have you forsaken me?' (Matt. 27.46). This is the death of which scripture speaks, associating it with a fundamental break which goes back to first beginnings when Adam, man, estranged himself from his intimate relationship with God and forfeited the possibility of passing peacefully towards immortal existence, experiencing 'no more than a natural and tranquil departure' (Péguy).

It is of this death that St Paul speaks in Romans:

' . . . by one man sin came into the world and by sin death, and thus death reached all men because all have sinned' (Rom. 5.12).

There is certainly a profound connection between the dramatic death of man and a fundamental guilt which has its roots in the original estrangement. That is what Christians have always known, because 'it was not like this at the beginning' (Matt. 19).

We have deliberately applied this saying of Christ about marriage to human death in order to bring out as strongly as possible the utter freedom with which Jesus spoke of the original cause of human death.

Thus Genesis 3 has this to say about the ultimate consequence of the fall of Adam and Eve: as a result of it, death became a tragedy.

Far from having exhausted all the riches of this narrative, we have done no more than try to bring out a way of reading it which avoids certain current errors of interpretation which are likely to discourage modern readers who know something about our scientific culture.

We hope to have demonstrated the inexhaustible anthropological significance of this text. It sheds light on an ongoing drama which unfolds over centuries and generations, increasingly illuminated by the victory of Christ, on the cross, over the one who, in the beginning, led human beings astray down the road of rejection and estrangement.

Any attempt to establish a direct relationship between time and space as reconstructed by modern palaeontology on the one hand and the episode of the fall on the other would not really mean anything, and so commentators rightly reject what they call concordism.

However, Christians will never abandon their quest through human history back to its most distant spiritual origins in an attempt to illuminate the drama that we continue to experience each day.

7

Evolution Towards What? The Future of Humanity

Many works of science fiction describe the future of evolution for us, but owe much more to imagination than to real knowledge. What can we say about humanity?

A reminder of past evolution

We have already looked at the origins of humanity, and this naturally leads us to ask about our future. First let us recall some of the essential points of the human adventure so far.

Humanity is an integral part of the living world; without any doubt we are the product of evolution, the rules of which also apply to us. Our appearance arises from processes analogous to those which presided over the progressive transformation of all other living species.

One axis emerges from this extraordinary long and complex history, extended over several thousand million years: the quest for increasing independence from the environment. This progressive liberation is represented by the acquisition of increasingly complex behaviour, supported by a central nervous system, which provides for increasingly developed coordination. This has enabled the world of vertebrates to take possession of the earth.

The basic lines of the human form were achieved as soon as the primate adopted an upright position, as soon as his hand became free and his skull was liberated from the constraining muscles needed by the quadruped. At this stage of anatomical organization, however, which was achieved by the first Australopitheci, human evolution had only just begun.

Biological and anatomical evolution has obviously gone on since then. The bodies of *homo erectus (pithecanthropos)*, of the first members of *homo sapiens*, and finally of the *homo sapiens sapiens* of the painted caves show these successive transformations.

Future evolution on a biological level

Is this biological evolution still continuing? The problem has often been discussed. We have no adequate perspective for appreciating it, since historical times have not yet lasted for ten millennia, and that is a very brief period given the overall length of evolution.

We can say little for certain about the anatomical and physiological aspects of human evolution. Some scientists argue that body hair has been reduced, supposing it to have been more important for our distant ancestors than for us; however, we have no precise information about the amount of body hair on these ancestors. Some scientists have argued that the little toe is disappearing or that our toes are becoming more joined together, but there is no serious reason for claiming this. It could be forecast that the human anatomy will implement all the consequences of upright stance, the primordial condition of our evolution, but some scientists think that virtually all these consequences have already been realized.

Be this as it may, comparing ourselves with our most recent prehistoric or even historic ancestors, we may note some interesting features. Thus from the period of the Lascaux paintings on, human beings like us, with round heads (*brachycephaloi* = short skulls), became increasingly numerous, while the proportion of those with long heads (*dolichocephaloi*) has increased. This was perhaps a last readjustment following the attainment of an upright stance.

Moreover, the proportion of modern men and women with 'wisdom teeth' (back molars) is decreasing, and this marks a certain reduction in the number of our teeth. The average height of individuals has increased since the Australopitheci; it still seems to be growing, at least among the populations of the rich countries. However, this growth may be specifically a consequence of improved diet rather than a genetic development.

All we can say is that minor changes and the anatomical study of human beings seem to show that the consequences of the upright stance can hardly be taken much further. The jaw has receded, but it cannot continue to do so much more without affecting the way we eat. The volume of the skull cannot increase much, because it is approaching its biological limits: the head has to be capable of being balanced without too much muscular effort and the birth of children cannot be excessively complicated.

On what level will the future of humanity develop?

So are we at the end of an evolutionary branch? Are we threatened with extinction, or shall we continue for a long time in our present state? In raising these long-term questions, there is one piece of evidence that we can no longer escape: the problem no longer arises in simple terms of palaeontological and biological evolution. Over human history, anatomical evolution would appear modest compared with the consequences of the extraordinary evolution of behaviour and the mind (though of course this is dependent on anatomical evolution). It is on this point that we need to concentrate in our reflections on the future of humanity. The upright ape introduced a new factor into the interplay of biological evolution. Future prognostications must take account of it. Hence the question raised by H. Tintant: 'Is man the product or the author of his evolution?'

For the human race, with its consciousness and its ascendancy over the surrounding world, has introduced, on a planetary scale, developments at a much more rapid pace than the slow rate of biological evolution. Without having time to evolve, in the biological sense of the term, human beings have been led to develop their capabilities considerably, to transmit them to descendants through culture, and constantly to increase the potential of their species for action and knowledge.

What new factors have human beings introduced as over against the rest of the biological world?

Every living species that 'evolves', that adapts itself to a new environment, does so by modifying its organism. This is naturally a very slow process, taking a number of successive generations. With human beings, by contrast, from the beginning artefacts in the broadest sense of the term (tools, clothing, places to live in) have taken

What future can they expect?   *Photo Pfalzer-Viollet*

the place of biological adaptations, opening up an almost indefinite range of resources, while human beings themselves are not physically changed by the process of adaptation. In some respects we are independent of this adaptation. Such independence from the increasing narrowness involved in physical specialization has allowed human beings to keep all their options open for a technological evolution based on the hand and the brain. And from now onwards it is at the heart of this technological evolution that an important part of the debate over selection, favouring the 'fittest' human beings, will take place. The adaptation of the human organism has been reduced to a minimum, but that does not mean that it has disappeared altogether; some populations are good examples of physiological evolution in terms of adaptation to a climate or environment (Eskimos, Pygmies and Nilotes); such adaptations are confined within the framework of biological evolution (which of course is very slow). Furthermore, we know that athletic training, particularly professional training, can shape the body and the reflexes in such a way as to improve the individual's performance. However, this training is always subject to the choice of the individual who engages in it; he or she can begin it, modify it or end it; and of course it has no hereditary effect.

However, what a human being has acquired once in one place can spread throughout his or her social group, be transmitted from generation to generation, and extend from one society to another in such a way as to reach the whole of humanity. This cultural tradition was originally oral, and then came to be based on written languages which allowed it to jump several generations; from now on it can be transmitted by broadcasts and audio-visual recordings, making it possible to reach large areas of the human race simultaneously and also to hand material down to generations to come. We thus have an unlimited cultural potential which will remain at our disposal to the degree in which we choose to take advantage of it, rather than being utterly preoccupied with everyday life.

105

The human ascendancy over nature

Thanks to our adaptation by means of artefacts, as human beings we can choose our environment and adapt it as a place to live in, overcoming problems posed by the natural environment. Thus we can travel through the air, in 'houses under the sea' and even in interplanetary space (human beings have walked on the moon and could doubtless go still further). On earth we can reduce external factors to a minimum: we can cope with cold and heat; we can cultivate the deserts.

Now the action of the natural environment plays a determinative role in the living world by allowing the existence of a selection which is one of the factors in biological evolution. Here, too, the human species tends to escape the common rule.

This attenuation of the role of selection in the human world by the interplay of a whole series of social and technological factors has important consequences. First, human beings can increasingly remedy various causes of early mortality (though this form of selection has by no means disappeared, since mortality in the embryo – spontaneous abortions – eliminates numerous mutations in chromosomes which are not viable). The result of that is an exponential growth in the world population. On the other hand, some more or less unfavourable 'mutations' are not eliminated regularly by selection, and this increases the number of individuals in the population handicapped by such mutations. From the point of view of evolution, this partial lifting of the pressure of selections slows down the diversification of populations. On the other hand, it has a positive aspect: the enrichment of the genetic potential of the human species by the conservation of mutations which would otherwise be lost. Even if these mutations are at first sight unfavourable, we are often unaware of their properties, and there are instances of habitually pernicious mutations which are beneficial in certain conditions. Nevertheless, this reduction of natural selection among human beings presents new problems to humanity, notably the demand to welcome and support the handicapped.

The development of manufacture to the point where it becomes industry in the modern sense of the term makes man the most 'onerous' of all the species in the living world. Man costs his environment dear. There is no other example in the living world of a species which requires so much energy and raw materials for the growth and support of each individual. This problem, unsuspected until a few decades ago, is widely recognized today. It will clearly reach a critical point in less than a century.

Human ascendancy over the human condition

However, human beings have increasingly refined means of coping with these various problems which have such serious consequences for our future. Thus we can use not only artefacts which are extensions of the hand 'outside the body', but also artefacts providing information which are as it were the external extension of the brain. Just as the mattock increases the efficiency of the hand, so the computer increases that of the human brain – to a degree which is still incalculable. Of course the computer is not a substitute for thought, nor is it innovative: it does not have, nor can it replace, the self-determination of the human individual, the faculty of choice in planning. But in numerous mental tasks it can not only replace the brain but also go far beyond the possibilities of a human brain, or even a number of brains working together. It offers us, with amazing rapidity, the results of numerous operations, remembering them and comparing them. The biological mutations that would be needed to achieve such efficiency are unimaginable. We are freeing ourselves from the limitations of our brains, or rather, relieving our brains of technical tasks so that we can think more quickly and plan much further ahead with a far greater knowledge of things.

We have also come to know our own biological condition with sufficient precision to be able to affect our physical state. The use of effective medicines is, of course, very old. But knowledge of our physiological and genetic mechanisms has now developed to such a degree that living organisms, bacteria, are already being used for the programmed manufacture of substances which play an important role in human physiology. We are beginning to manipulate biological mechanisms. Scientists are moving cautiously, and with difficulty, towards an increasingly precise control of such mechanisms. Those with imagination are already forecasting the day when scientists can not just act on particular mechanisms in isolation, but can also control and orientate human evolution. Biologists know that we are still far from such dreams (or nightmares), but we are living at a time when these dreams are being dreamed; and they are a very urgent challenge to us to see that we become highly responsible human beings.

In fact it would seem that we shall be able to discover the natural laws which have given us our existence. It is not out of the question that we shall be able to intervene in these laws; it is already certain that we will be able to use them. Following such an emancipation from the environment, from material constraints and even from certain limitations on our own biological nature, our new quest can only be in the direction of much greater responsibility, greater freedom, enabling us to choose better.

Human freedom and a sense of limitation

Contrary to what nineteenth-century scientists believed, the development of science does not make either philosophy or religion superfluous. This development does, however, make it all the more necessary than ever that they should be as profound as possible. Only by profound searching can we arrive at the answer which we seek, at that extra spiritual dimension which is an indispensable counter-balance to the increasing material progress which is being achieved by science.

It is particularly important that we should not be enslaved by our material progress, that we should remain free in the face of all the conditioning which our industry imposes on us. Paul's warning, 'Be sober', is truer than ever. For there is no way in which as human beings we can ever escape the limits of our own persons: we cannot yield to all the external pressures with which our technology assails us and at the same time remain free to pursue our own way of life.

Human beings aspire to overcome all their limitations, to know now, to be able to do everything. Our dreams, our legends and myths express the infinity of our desires with our finite means and capacities. In terms of our biological nature, as individuals we die, like all biological beings. But unlike other living beings, we have acquired an awareness, a freedom, in which we can perceive our limits: not only the limits of our means, of our strength, but also the limits of our existence as mortal, biological beings. Naturally inclined to reject this deceptive limitation, we try to escape it.

There are some ways in which it is partly possible to escape our finite limitations. We transcend the limits imposed on us by the lapse of time in part by our plans and visions, and in part by the testimonies which have come down to us from people of the past. The works of art from antiquity and prehistory prove in some degree to be resistant to time. Nor is that all: the formation of all human beings, the construction of their personalities, depends on the legacy of human past handed down to us through culture. Those who handed down this cultural legacy are dead, but something of them remains in their descendants. Of course, animal species manifest a degree of 'immortality' by virtue of the perpetuation of their reproductive cells; but this is no more than an automatic and unconscious transmission of genetic characteristics. While human beings still have some sense of this type of partial immortality (see the idea of posterity in antiquity and in the Old Testament), they have also developed a new type of immortality, again partial, but now concerned not only with the species but also with the individual. This 'immortality' resides in the richness of a cultural heritage, the objective reality of the deposit of thought contained in it, the discovery of love which leaves each person an heir to humanity as it progresses by means of an ongoing legacy accumulated and refashioned as generation gives way to generation. Thus present-day men and women are the product of the accumulation and assimilation of riches carried down as a deposit by the history of humanity.

If we wanted to start humanity all over again from two babies, one a boy and one a girl, brought up without any contact with other human beings, it would be impossible for them to produce humanity as it is today, despite their genes. All they could arrive at would be a very early stage, before all the cultures of *homo sapiens*. And even that presupposes that they had succeeded in surviving and producing descendants, which is far from being certain.

If animal death might seem to be the price paid for an evolution accelerated by the succession of generations, human death would seem to be the price paid for this cultural 'immortality' in which the person attains a certain resonance in following generations (among people outside his or her own descendants). Here we have a perpetuation, a progression, which transcends the bounds of a particular human life. This progression impels men and women to hope for their future. They form desires for this future and shape dreams, myths, which correspond to their aspirations. They practise burial rites which express their deep sense of a need to go beyond death. Putting questions to computers programmed for limited and therefore reassuring responses, men and women try to evaluate the distance which still separates them from the victory over death for which they hope; for death remains the prime symbol – and the specific mark – of all our limitations. People dream of using the means provided by ongoing progress to transcend all that binds them to their mortal state. Everyone has entertained the idea of a better form of existence in one way or the other,

depending on his or her capacity to conceive of this better form of existence and consciously aspire to it.

However, reality compels us to recognize that there is no doing away with our main human limitations: not just death, but also the evil which makes us turn against ourselves and destroys us. We may have proved successful in warding off illness, but we cannot ward off old age and death. The most elaborate scientific means may give us a bit more time, but they cannot banish death from our organisms. It is built into them from the very beginning. Scientific means may give us the possibility of improving our lot during our lifetime, but there is nothing in science which can make someone's innermost conscience concerned for the good of fellow human beings. On the contrary, the most sophisticated developments of technology are open to all human beings, whatever their character, and those who use these developments for hate and destruction often seem to be the most enterprising.

The Creator

The one God whom we adore is Father, Son and Spirit; he is not alone. He did not create us to relieve his solitude. It is not as if we had been made to amuse a deity in his boredom. It is through disinterested love that he calls us to existence.

Nor is it through need that he saves us in his own Son, or that he unites us to himself by his own Spirit; it is through sheer goodness, in the generosity of his love for us. He has made all things out of nothing. All that we are, all that we have, we receive continually from him.

The Bishops of France

Are we then reduced to a philosophy of the absurd, as many thinkers claim? But if we are, why this call to life, to eternity, which we feel to be addressed to us? Is that of no account? That is hardly the view held by anyone who believes in the reality of a higher state. But if that is the case, why should we refuse to recognize that what we discover within ourselves is a real need, an aspiration the object of which is capable of filling our whole being?

From death to Easter

That certainly leads us to recognize the existence of realities which cannot be reduced to knowledge of a scientific type. Of course such a conclusion does not mean that we repudiate scientific knowledge. We still need scientific knowledge in order to understand the world, and often it illuminates the faith of believers. What we have to do, rather, is resolutely to adopt a metaphysical and religious perspective which, without rejecting science, on the whole takes a different course.

Closely bound up with our freedom, this aspiration to a higher state that is to be found among human beings represents an absolute demand which is a natural feature of all freedom. A partial freedom, like the one we have, aspires to grow without limit.

It is at that point that we need to look at the origins of freedom. Is it the unique result of an evolutionary process which, starting from inanimate matter, forms conscious beings and leads them towards boundless freedom? What would such boundless freedom be? How could it have emerged from a material evolutionary process had it not existed there from the beginning? If this boundless freedom exists, it is prior to all else. Freedom, then, is creative; it is at the source of being, the source of evolution, the source of life, the source of our awareness, of our vocation to life and unbounded liberty.

Now if this boundless freedom is a God limited by neither time nor space, human reason is not negated, but is called on to discover an unfathomable mystery of which only the believer has some experience. This God cannot but be unique; otherwise he would be limited by others, or at least kept from an intimate union with these others which would lead to unity. And our freedom is just one fragment of this boundless freedom which attracts us, as the goal of our existence.

The profundity of our human aspiration to transcend our limits, to transcend death, corresponds to our image of God, an image which expresses our need of the object which is the source of this image. Dreams of the infinite and the eternal which haunt men and women seem in a way to be premonitions. The transition from these dreams to the reality of the infinite and of eternity is like moving up to the level of the Creator; and this is only possible if the Creator intervenes, by entering into dialogue with humanity and raising men and women to the status of his conversation partner. For human beings cannot attain total liberty without becoming united to the one who is himself liberty, the One who Is. This union is clearly possible only through the initiative of the One who Is, and we are left free to accept it.

Now it is of the specific possibility of this union that the Bible tells us. On the one hand creation shows us an omnipotent God, beyond the constraints of human vicissitudes, since by nature he is the One who Is, and does not depend on anything. On the other hand the biblical revelation shows us a God involved with his creatures, a God offended and suffering from offences committed against him. For this God did not wish to act as an omnipotent and inaccessible manipulator of this creation. On the contrary, it was his will to enter into his creation, to take the risk of dialogue with his free creature. From the beginning of his dialogue with humanity, God offered us life in covenant with him, a response to the human need to be united to the very source of being and freedom. However, refusing to find their fulfilment in the Creator and demanding to make their own definitions of good and evil, human beings rejected this first covenant. So it came about that God (the Good Shepherd) restored our human chances of attaining his life and freedom through a series of covenants which were often betrayed (men and women as the lost sheep for whom he searches, even to the point of suffering death).

God willed to involve himself in the world, to suffer rejection and hatred. He willed to absorb all human evil into himself in order to annihilate it. So it is that he made himself human, since in human form he could suffer for humanity, be our partner in dialogue without annihilating us, share our condition to the point of sharing our death. For it is by God's own will that he became Christ, came as one among us, came to the world of human beings to offer them the possibility of living his life, even suffering death for us in order to plant this life there. The apparent failure of the death of Christ repelled the men and women of his time as it still repels those of ours, unless they see that this death is itself the fulfilment of

God creating the sun and the moon. La Sainte Chappelle. *Photo Viollet*

The Creative Act

The creative act is not interpolated in the chain of antecedents. It is imposed upon the universe taken in its full extension and full duration.

It is impossible, therefore, for the elements of the world to emerge from the world, to reach even a lower limit of the world. It is impossible for it to conceive (logically) a physical term for the world, or even (rationally) to imagine the isolated creation of an element of the world apart from or outside it. All around us, until it is lost to sight, radiates the net of spatial and temporal series, endless and untearable, so closely woven in one piece that there is not one single knot in it that does not depend upon the whole fabric.

God did not will individually (nor could he have constructed as though they were separate bits) the sun, the earth, plants, or Man. He willed his Christ; – and in order to have his Christ, he had to create the spiritual world, and man in particular, upon which Christ might germinate; and to have man, he had to launch the vast process of organic life (which, accordingly, is not a superfluity but an essential organ of the world); and the birth of that organic life called for the entire cosmic turbulence.

Pierre Teilhard de Chardin,
Science and Christ, Collins and Harper 1968, p.79

Christ's mission, previously willed and foretold (by the prophets and by Christ himself). This is how the life of God was introduced into the death of men and women, invading death itself with divine life in such a way that where life had had no access there was no longer life, and 'death should be no more' (Rev. 21.4.).

And yet the human death of Christ is very real, so real that many people cannot see more than that: it was important for this reality to be seen clearly. However, Christ's death itself contains his victory, as is shown by the Eastern icons. It is by dying on the cross that Christ conquers evil and death. The manifestation of this victory is deferred by several days – otherwise the death would not be seen to be real. The resurrection which manifests the victory of Christ in his passage through death, in his Passover, is not universally visible, for God does not obliterate our freedom by overwhelming divine acts. It was shown to those who had believed in Jesus but had not expected this resurrection, since they had not understood the warnings of the Lord. The fact that the state of the Risen Christ is of such a nature as to be beyond the precise control of our senses – which are necessarily bypassed by a supernatural phenomenon – does not prevent him from being able to show himself to us.

However, the reality of the resurrection can begin to take possession of us without our waiting for its bodily realization. That is what matters today and directs our future.

Freedom and resurrection

By implanting life in human death, Christ destroys this death. Of course physical death continues to force itself on us, marking a transition from our world as harsh as it is necessary; however, its subjective significance is now completely different, since it is no longer annihilation but a transition. It is no longer an end, since we have attained a resurrection.

Christ also destroys evil in his death, not, this time, by becoming involved in it, since God remains a stranger to evil, but by bearing it, absorbing in himself all the evil that human beings could inflict on him, covering himself with our sins even to the point of being marked with them. Christ absorbs all this evil and drowns it in his love. It is the suffering and death of Christ that make sense of the passionate words and complaints addressed by the God of the Old Testament to his people and to humanity; for it is in Christ that the suffering of God is realized.

However, this death of Christ is also the expression of the most utter freedom: leading the whole of his human life in a way aimed at saving men and women by offering them union in a new and definitive covenant, Christ no longer allows himself to be dissuaded by any obstacle or any fear. He makes his death itself the fulfilment of his mission. The resurrection expresses this total freedom, breaking even the bounds of death.

Christians will shape their future on a growing union with Christ. Not only will they receive the good news of Christ, who has come to bring them life (eternal life), but they will convey this good news to all people, since the message now passes through each individual Christian to the world. By adopting Christ's own attitudes and conduct in their human life, Christians will unite themselves to him and, by this union, begin to enter on the beginnings of resurrection in the total freedom of God. They can in fact hope to free themselves progressively from psychological conditioning, human inclinations and passions, since God's plan and God's love, which will guide their behaviour, transcend these inclinations and passions. All this is put well in St Paul's letters (Eph. 2.3-6; Col. 2.12-13; Col. 3.1-4; Rom. 6.4-11, 22-23).

Moreover, Christian behaviour will also follow that of Christ in the face of evil. Instead of letting evil rebound on to others, passing it on from one person to another, causing more and more damage, Christians will absorb it and try to drown it in the love which God gives them. That does not hold out prospects of an easy future, but it is the way in which each one of us, progressively, can build up the resurrection through the different stages of the cross that we undergo. What we shall find here is a growth in freedom, for the tension arising from our relationship with God will give us a sovereign freedom over against our conditioning and whatever may tempt us. Such a prospect is clearly an ideal one, and Christian behaviour does not consistently attain this level. However, it can at least move in this direction; and history gives us numerous examples of men and women who have attained, each in his or her own way, in accordance with their vocation, a form of this divine freedom. Such people have been called saints; some of them, like St Francis of Assisi, are famed for the harmony that they have manifested with the whole of creation.

However, Christians have a heavy responsibility, since they also bear the good news of Christ. How can others recognize the good news if those who bear it do not seem to live it out? For God calls all men and women, and so many people do not seem to hear his good news; they cannot be accused of always being deaf to his

---

St Paul and Resurrection in the Life of Christ

Ephesians 2.4-6
But God, who is rich in mercy, out of the great love with which he loved us, even when we were dead through our trespasses, made us alive together with Christ (by grace you have been saved), and raised us up with him, and made us sit with him in the heavenly places in Christ Jesus.

Colossians 2.12-13
And you were buried with him in baptism, in which you were also raised with him through faith in the working of God, who raised him from the dead. And you, who were dead in trespasses and the uncircumcision of your flesh, God made alive together with him, having forgiven us all our trespasses.

Colossians 3.1-4
If then you have been raised with Christ, seek the things that are above, where Christ is, seated at the right hand of God. Set your minds on things that are above, not on things that are on earth. For you have died, and your life is hid with Christ in God. When Christ who is our life appears, then you also will appear with him in glory.

Romans 6.4-11
We were buried therefore with him by baptism into death, so that as Christ was raised from the dead by the glory of the Father, we too might walk in newness of life. For if we have been united with him in a death like his, we shall certainly be united with him in a resurrection like his. We know that our old self was crucified with him so that the sinful body might be destroyed, and we might no longer be enslaved to sin. For he who has died is freed from sin. But if we have died with Christ, we believe that we shall also live with him. For we know that Christ being raised from the dead will never die again; death no longer has dominion over him. The death he died to sin, once for all, but the life he lives he lives to God. So you also must consider yourselves dead to sin and alive to God in Christ Jesus.

Romans 6.22-23
But now that you have been set free from sin and have become slaves of God, the return you get is sanctification and its end, eternal life. For the wages of sin is death, but the free gift of God is eternal life in Christ Jesus our Lord.

voice, since those who transmit it do not always do so clearly. Moreover, God chooses the time for each of us, and that is something that we do not know.

Now God does not expect a person to recognize him before he acts. He has already put into every human heart a desire for justice and love, and this is often expressed by those who are not believers. They too can bear his message. God is present in all human behaviour which responds to the demands of justice and love, as he is present in all that is conformed to him, even if those in whom he is present are not aware of the fact (cf. Rom. 2.14f.; 2.26). Many people who seek God sincerely do not believe that they have found him because his presence does not correspond to the criteria of majesty and omnipotence (and even of magical power) which Christian opinion often puts forward. Real though these criteria are, they are not the only ones, and God sometimes chooses to enter into human life in a different way. When you defend the weak, when you give food to the hungry, when you fight and suffer for justice and peace, when you are a brother or sister to those in need. . . You may not have been aware of the fact, but this desire in you was God touching you; for what you did, you did for him (cf. Matt. 25.37-40; cf. also Tobit 12.13-14).

Chapter 2 has shown us how organic death was a requisite for rapid evolutionary progress over a series of generations. So we can take this biological event as a parable: the living being comes into existence through organic death and through organic death it leaves room for its descendants, in whom evolutionary progress can go further. This first image of the dialectic between death and resurrection becomes more significant when the death is human, i.e. not just organic death but also a subjective drama in which the conscious being is brought face to face with the totally unknown, the other world (even if the being concerned expects only nothingness). It is by undergoing this death that the human individual bequeathes to future humanity his or her own contribution to cultural development (even though at the time that may be quite unknown). This death is not yet of itself an Easter; that calls for a fully conscious and totally free attitude of the kind that was to be found in Christ Jesus. It is when it has the character of free acceptance, an awareness of going to God, that human death is paschal; and when that happens, it too hands on something of the message of Christ.

So death and human suffering can take on an Easter meaning, just as the pains of childbirth give rise to a new life. The future of humanity is not just the future of the species but also the future of people called to fulfil their freedom in joint responsibility with the Creator. And are human beings the only form of life concerned with this new being? If we reflect on Romans (8.18-22), we may dream that there is much still to be discovered about the whole of creation.

The Glory to Come

I consider that the sufferings of the present time are not worth comparing with the glory that is to be revealed to us. For the creation waits with eager longing for the revealing of the sons of God: for the creation was subjected to futility, not of its own will, but by the will of him who subjected it in hope; because the creation itself will be set free from its bondage to decay and obtain the glorious liberty of the children of God. We know that the whole creation has been groaning in travail together until now.

(Rom. 8.18-22)

How to Read the World

We have now come to the end of this brief study, which was meant to be a piece of interdisciplinary research into the adventure of life and evolution up to and including man, and also a sketch of the historical and spiritual future of humanity. So now is the time to ask whether our enterprise has been successful and what conclusions can be drawn.

We hope that we have demonstrated the profound unity of the phenomena of life, evolution, and the emergence of man, whose originality cannot be reduced to anything else in nature.

At the level of a phenomenological reading, there is no stage at which we have seen the appearance of a radical break, of outside intervention, or of the action of any non-terrestrial agent.

Only other readings of the same phenomena, made in the light of a specific anthropological view of man which includes a spiritual experience, allow us to discern the creative presence of God; this is invisible, and we can only see its effects.

We have not tried to put any pressure on you, our readers. We have simply invited you to see evolution as the manifestation of the Creator God who makes humanity with a view to a covenant of love which will be sealed definitively in his Son. For us, that means that beyond all the mechanisms of physics and chemistry which seem logically to lead matter to structure itself in living organisms, there is a global meaning to this adventure culminating in man which can only be the will of the God of love.

God is the One who at every moment allows every being, indeed the whole cosmos, to exist; without him nothing that exists would exist. We have no difficulty in accepting the statement about the Logos made by St John: 'All things were made by him and without him was not anything made that was made' (John 1.3).

Of course, even without this statement it is possible to have a sound general understanding of the emergence of man in the cosmos. But it lacks an essential key, the one which gives us the secret of the universe, the revelation of the light which lightens our darkness, which shows where and when we have a revelation, at the heart of his work, of the One who, with the Father, is its source.

Not to know that is like admiring a beautiful picture without knowing where the painter's signature is.

Not to know that is not to know that the adventure of life has its source in the love of the Three Persons and only finds its fulfilment in this same love.

Of course we recognize that some readers will be able to accept that there is a creative presence – and even exclaim with the Psalmist, 'How great are your works, O Lord!' (Ps.92) – without necessarily believing in the incarnation of the creative word in Jesus of Nazareth. That is the faith of Jews and Muslims, and it is the root of our own faith.

However, we think that all the activity of Jesus, like his teaching, reveals to us the truth of what St John says: 'The Word was made flesh and dwelt among us' (John 1.14).

Risen, he is among us acting at the heart of his church and beyond, and his action guides in a mysterious way the human and spiritual future of humanity.

It is in the light of Christ and the Spirit given at Pentecost that we want to reflect on some aspects of our human vocation to participate in the creative work of his Father.

Work

All human labour can perhaps be read as the extension and development of the divine saying, 'subdue the earth'. A recent encyclical of Pope John Paul II develops this theme at length.

Before man, the creative activity of God was manifested through physical and chemical mechanisms which allowed the slow development of structures leading to living matter and the long process by which it became more complex.

With the appearance of humanity, and above all with the development of skills, followed by the birth of modern technology, a connecting

Serve the Creator: Rule over Creation

We receive our being from the Father through the Son as a free gift and a task entrusted to our hands; we also receive the world as a great body given to us to respect and to build up. Instead of fettering us, belief in the Creator assures us of our true freedom. If God is the source and the sole judge of our freedom, no force on earth has the right to enslave us.

Since creation thus denotes a living relationship, constantly upheld, between the creature and his Creator, the meaning and value of our work are illuminated in a remarkable way. The human activity, individual and collective, by which men and women down the centuries have tried to improve the conditions in which they live, is in accordance with God's design. Men and women, created in the image of God, have been given the task of ordering the earth and all that it contains, and of organizing family, social and political relationships. By recognizing God as the creator of all things, we are called to submit ourselves and the universe to him, so that the very name of God may be glorified throughout the earth. God is the master of time and history; he is the one who makes fruitful the work of our hands and the creations of our minds. In the love which he bestows on us, he allows the fruits of eternity to ripen in history. By fulfilling creation, men and women fulfil themselves.

Despite the shocks of history, despite the scandal of suffering and death, we refuse to be turned aside from God. Through all our trials we hold fast to the faith that God is right to give us life, to send his Son to save the world, to fill it with his Spirit of holiness and communion. Set as we are in this world, we find in it a high vocation: to live together as sons united in the Son, called to make all creation a place where brothers and sisters live together.

The Bishops of France

link was established between God and his creation in the form of prehistoric man and then modern man. The human race began to attain powers which could be used to shape the universe in accordance with God's aims.

This connecting link was embodied in God's own Son, who for almost thirty years worked at a manual trade. That is how the church can proclaim the 'gospel of work', because God himself has worked at a human trade (as John Paul II's encyclical points out).

Man, who could never have the power to be his own originator or to be the originator of the universe, nevertheless exercises a royal ministry in his work, by organizing the world, dominating it, and trying to make justice, peace and love prevail there. He shares directly, but as a creature, in the work of creation. He becomes an active agent in the transformation of the world and plays an increasingly conscious and responsible role in this genesis, which began several thousand million years ago. According to a phrase of P. Varillon, 'he was created creator'.

Human beings can grow in this mastery and this conquest if they can show sufficient wisdom to dominate the forces of 'decreation', those which contribute to the disorganization and the death of the species. The new power which is now in our hands gives us a new and in some respects terrifying responsibility. Not only our biological evolution but the very future of our species depends on whether or not we can control our power. The future of other living species also depends on us; they are bound up with us in a future of development or in the destruction which we can bring down on them.

The sphere of procreation can serve as an illustration of this new responsibility.

Procreation

If there is one mystery of life where human beings feel themselves profoundly involved in the creative work of God it is that of 'procreation'. Of course we need to get rid of the simplistic idea that the parents only create the body of the child and that in addition God endows it with a soul.

We believe that from the time when the human ovum is fertilized by the free act of two persons united in love, a human being exists even if he or she is not yet fully human. Everything is the gift of God; everything is the gift of the parents; but not in the same way. God brings into existence a new being, called to be his child, through the decision of the parents and by the biological means of a fertilized ovum. The root source of the child's existence is the creative fatherhood of God, but that cannot come about apart from the agency of two free beings who, by giving themselves to each other, choose to make their love fruitful and to bring into existence an unknown being who will be their child.

God has created the child: so have the parents, but in a different way, since they receive their existence from God at every moment, and that includes the very freedom to be fertile. The word 'procreation' marks this difference, but we must avoid understanding it as a simple sharing of tasks: part for God and part for men and women.

The human being, body and soul (some people find this distinction difficult to manage) had his or her existence wholly from parents and wholly from God, though that is not to mention later relationships which will in fact make him or her a person. No one is only 'partly' involved, for example the parents in the body and God in the soul. God is the origin of all that we are, and is so at every moment.

Now the new mastery of humanity over the process of fertilization, like the new situation represented by a population explosion which is the nightmare of governments in Third-World countries, produces the need to explore new ways of arriving at a dynamic of reasonable growth for people and populations. Both anthropological and theological reflection must ceaselessly wrestle with these new factors in the light received from God for his loving plan for humanity. Here we shall simply point to a vast area in which numerous specialists in humane and religious sciences are already at work.

Called to give life by the one who gave them existence and the very power to choose, men and women discover themselves in Christ the Son, irresistibly impelled by the Spirit to offer the world in a liturgy of thanksgiving, and to offer themselves in a constant sacrifice of love.

Offering and thanksgiving

Following other writers, but with his own touch of brilliance, Teilhard de Chardin in his 'Mass on the World' offered to God 'the growth of the world borne ever onwards in the stream of universal becoming'.

Rediscovering ancient actions, older than the religion of Israel, derived from the offering of the first fruits, he was impelled by his priestly love to make the same gesture as the Son: to give back to the Father what he had received from the Father. At the heart of the world one can only hear this incessant prayer made by the Son in the Spirit.

Teilhard translates it like this:

Since once again, Lord – though this time not in the forests of the Aisne but in the steppes of Asia – I have neither bread, nor wine, nor altar, I will raise myself beyond these symbols, to the pure majesty of the real itself; I, your priest, will make the whole earth my altar and on it will offer you all the labours and sufferings of the world. . .

Receive, O Lord, this all-embracing host which your whole creation, moved by your magnetism, offers you at this dawn of a new day.

This bread, our toil, is of itself, I know, but an immense fragmentation; this wine, our pain, is no more, I know, than a draught which dissolves. Yet in the very depths of the formless mass you have implanted – and this I am sure of, for I sense it – a desire, irresistible, hallowing, which makes us cry out, believer and unbeliever alike: 'Lord, make us one.'

(*Hymn of the Universe*, Collins and Harper 1965; Fount 1977, pp.19f.).

Here is a man, illuminated by the Spirit of God, who feels himself impelled to offer the world and to give thanks, in a ceaseless eucharist, for what is the adventure of the creation to come. Not to see creation in these terms is to deprive it of its most fundamental dimension: the permanent praise of God, which is proclaimed by the Psalmist: 'The heavens are telling the glory of God.' To obstruct this praise is to keep creation a prisoner of vanity (Rom. 8.19) and therefore to keep entire peoples oppressed by ideological or spiritual tyranny.

Life created by God calls for a new creation;
captive realities, for a liberation;
that which is subjected to the prince of lies,
    for a redemption.

Such is the nature of the world which strives to praise and give thanks while living in moral and spiritual captivity.

From eucharist to communion

All that we need to finish this outline is to express once again the innermost concerns of every human being.

Called to thanksgiving, we are called to loving fellowship between ourselves and all men. The unity of matter, the very unity of the phenomenon of life, the unity of the human species, the unity of each individual, the desire for deep inter-personal relationships which exists in everyone, call for universal communion between all men and women. While there is great unanimity in noting this desire, people differ very widely over how it is to be obtained.

Although this book is not the place to give the reasons, for us Christians it seems clear that the way of unity among human beings on the one hand and unity between human beings and the whole of life on the other lies in the doctrine and the very person of Jesus, who died for the love of men and women and came to life again, acting at the heart of this world.

By his spirit, slowly over the centuries a communion of love has come into being which far transcends Christian confessions and other

religions. We call this the building up of the body of Christ.

> *For in him all the fullness of God was pleased to dwell, and through him to reconcile to himself all things, whether on earth or in heaven, making peace by the blood of his cross (Col. 1.19-20).*

> *There is one body and one Spirit, just as you were called to the one hope that belongs to your call, one Lord, one faith, one baptism, one God and Father of us all who is above all and through all and in all (Eph. 4.4-6).*

These two quotations from St Paul are sufficiently explicit for us not to have to stress a well-known aspect of Christian thought.

It takes a long time and much tenderness to make a person in God's image

Fulfilment in the total Christ

It remains for us to show what is perhaps a less well-known aspect of Christian thought relating to the spiritual and definitive future of humanity which is to come, i.e. the fulfilment of creation in the total Christ, head and body. This is Christ understood as the one who fills all things – what the Greek New Testament calls the *pleroma*.

Two biblical quotations will guide us here. We should meditate on the whole of the hymn to Christ, head of the universe, in the Letter to the Colossians, and especially this passage:

All things were created through him and for him. He is before all things, and in him all things hold together. He is the head of the body, the church (Col. 1.16-18).

For in him all the fullness of God was pleased to dwell. . . (Col. 1.19).

What is this mysterious fullness?

Some people see it as the 'universe filled with the presence of God'. The Old Testament already announced this fulfilment of the universe when Isaiah said, 'the earth shall be filled with the knowledge of the Lord as the waters cover the sea' (Isa. 11.9).

For us Christians, there will only be true fullness and fulfilment of the adventure of life and more particularly of humanity when God has invaded with his presence the whole body of humanity, transcending generations and millennia.

That will definitively come about only after the final restoration of human unity, i.e. the resurrection of the body at the time of the glorious final manifestation of the risen Christ (Matt. 25.31-46).

However, our world is no longer that of the New Testament, with its tiny pastoral representations of the end of the time. Our world is no longer the stabilized world of Newton. Our world has become a continually expanding giant of which we know only one tiny planet, lost in a galaxy among others. It is the scene of the extraordinary emergence of life, tending towards the burgeoning of human freedom and awareness dynamically influenced by the Spirit of God. We know through the words of Christ and of St Paul that all things are converging towards a unity of love which will only be definitive at the general resurrection of all men. We know that all will be fulfilled in the total Christ, the one whose body the church has grown amazingly over the past three centuries, above all with the population explosion and the recent discovery of the hitherto unknown depths of the history of humanity over past millennia.

At some moments our faith may be on the verge of tottering into the abyss if it gives way to the vertigo of the infinities of time and space.

Could Christ, since his birth in Galilee, have lost control of the universe as it now discloses itself with the vast dimensions of which we are aware today?

Does not the image of the total Christ revealed to us by St Paul seem minuscule beside the one sensed by countless Christians today?

The Omega Point

This proposition may seem very far-fetched; but the universe cannot be thought of as fully meeting the requirements, both extrinsic and intrinsic, of anthropogenesis unless it takes on the form of a convergent psychic milieu. It must necessarily reach its fulfilment, ahead of us, in some pole of super-consciouness in which all the personalized grains of consciousness survive and 'super-live'. It culminates in an Omega Point.

Pierre Teilhard de Chardin, *Science and Christ*, p.163

Christ the Evolver

Again physically and literally, the Christ is he who consummates: the plenitude of the world being finally effected only in the final synthesis in which a supreme consciousness will appear upon total, supremely organized, complexity. And since he, Christ, is the organic principle of this harmonizing process, the whole universe is *ipso facto* stamped with his character, shaped according to his direction, and animated by his form.

Finally and once more physically and literally, since all the structural lines of the world converge upon him and are knitted together in him, it is he who gives its consistence to the entire edifice of matter and Spirit. In him too, 'the head of Creation', it follows, the fundamental cosmic process of cephalization culminates and is completed, on a scale that is universal and with a depth that is supernatural, and yet in harmony with the whole of the past.

We see, then, that there is indeed no exaggeration in using the term Super-Christ to express that excess of greatness assumed in our consciousness by the Person of Christ in step with the awakening of our minds to the super-dimensions of the world and of mankind.

It is not, I insist, another Christ: it is the same Christ, still and always the same, and even more so in that it is precisely in order to retain for him his essential property of being co-extensive with the world that we are obliged to make him undergo this colossal magnification.

Christ-Omega: the Christ, therefore, who animates and gathers up all the biological and spiritual energies developed by the universe. Finally, then, Christ the evolver.

It is in that form then, now clearly defined and all-embracing, that Christ the Redeemer and Saviour henceforth offers himself for our worship.

Pierre Teilhard de Chardin, *Science and Christ*,

p. 167

On the other hand, many Christians never get beyond the dimensions of the tiny, domestic representations of the fulfilment of our history in terms of a rural Galilee.

Many others hesitate between doubt, disarray or utter speechlessness.

One man took the risk of describing what he felt to be the spiritual future of humanity in terms which went beyond the correct but excessively narrow representations in ancient scripture. This was a man who dissociated himself from excessively individualistic interpretations of his writing entitled 'The Mass on the World'; a man who was a prophet, priest and man of science, and whom we shall quote once again.

For Teilhard, the prodigious cosmogenesis whose spiritual and 'amorizing' dimensions we have been able to discern, can only be fulfilled in the universal Christ, the total Christ, the Omega point.

> We may dig things over as much as we please, but the universe cannot have two heads – it cannot be 'bicephalic'. The universal Christic centre, determined by theology, and the universal cosmic centre postulated by anthropogenesis: these two focal points ultimately coincide (or at least overlap) in the historical setting in which we are contained. Christ would not be the sole Mover, the sole Issue, of the universe if it were possible for the universe in any way to integrate itself, even to a lesser degree, apart from Christ. . .
>
> All the improbabilities disappear and St Paul's boldest sayings readily take on a literal meaning . . . when Christ, in virtue of his Incarnation, is recognized as carrying out precisely the functions of Omega (*Science and Christ*, pp.165,166).

Our faith then rediscovers its vigour and equilibrium. Instead of trembling before the new immensities of the universe, it learns to read in it the new dimensions of what must become the body of Christ.

Our prayer and our praise are fed on the very sap of the universe depending on the degree to

Teilhard de Chardin: Man of Faith and Religious Thought

On 18 May 1981, a colloquium was held at the Institut Catholique in Paris, presided over by Mgr Paul Poupard, to celebrate the centenary of the birth of Fr Teilhard de Chardin. This is the letter which Cardinal Casaroli wrote on the occasion of this event:

Vatican, 12 May 1981

Monsignor,

The international scientific community and indeed the whole of the scholarly world is preparing to celebrate the centenary of the birth of Fr Teilhard de Chardin. The amazing resonance of his works, along with the influence of his personality and the richness of his thought, have left an indelible stamp on our times.

Pierre Teilhard de Chardin combined a powerful poetic intuition into the profound significance of nature, a keen insight into the dynamism of creation and a broad vision of the future of the world with an undeniable religious fervour.

Similarly, his continual concern for dialogue with the science of his time and his intrepid optimism in the face of the evolution of the world meant that his intuitions attracted a great deal of attention through the sheen of his words and the magic of his imagery.

Orientated completely on the future, this synthesis, expressed in often lyrical terms and steeped in a passion for the universal, will have contributed to reviving hope in men and women prone to doubt.

However, at the same time, the complexity of the problems Fr Teilhard de Chardin touched on and the variety of approaches he used inevitably raised difficulties which rightly demand a critical and leisured study of his extraordinary work – on a scientific, as well as a philosophical and theological level.

There is no doubt that the celebrations of the centenary at the Institut Catholique or the Museum of Natural History in Paris, at UNESCO and at Notre Dame, will in this respect be a stimulating meeting of minds, contributing towards an exact methodology which will help towards the most rigorous epistomological investigation.

Beyond question, our age will remember, over and above the difficulties in the thought of this bold attempt at synthesis and the deficiencies in its expression, the witness of the integrity of a man seized by Christ in the depths of his being, who was concerned to respect faith and reason together, answering as it were in advance to the call of Jean Paul II: 'Have no fear, open wide to Christ the gates leading to the vast domains of culture, civilization and development.'

I am happy, Monsignor, to give you this message in the name of the Holy Father, for all those participating in the Colloquium at the Institut Catholique of Paris in honour of Fr Teilhard de Chardin of which you are presiding, and send you my warmest good wishes.

Agostino Cardinal Casaroli

which they allow themselves to be penetrated by the divine energies, the fire of the Holy Spirit which is slowly kindled in all those who are ready to be open to it. The greater the universe and the world of humanity proves to be in space and time, the more we praise God for his power and his love. And the more we bless him for having been born humbly in Galilee, of Mary, and for having spoken to us so simply a language which all, particularly the least among us, can understand. Cosmic vertigo is dangerous only for those who have not discovered the face of Christ.

In the guise of a tiny babe in its mother's arms, obeying the great law of birth, you came, Lord Jesus, to swell in my infant soul; and then, as you re-enacted in me – and in so doing extended the range of – your growth through the church, that same humanity which once was born and dwelt in Palestine began now to spread out gradually everywhere. . .

And all this took place because, in a universe which was disclosing itself to me as structurally convergent, you, by right of your resurrection, had assumed the domination position of all-inclusive Centre in which everything is gathered together. (Teilhard de Chardin, *The Heart of Matter*, Collins and Harcourt, Brace Jovanovich 1978, pp.55f.).

The final revelation

It is the purpose of the mysterious little book called Revelation, *Apocalypse*, the Greek word which means unveiling, and not the final catastrophe, as in current terminology, to reveal to us the future of the prodigious adventure of man from the time of his appearance on our planet more than two million years ago. In language which is as symbolic and rich as that in Genesis, it reveals to us the final triumph of Christ and all those who are faithful to him. The new creation fulfils the first and shows the extraordinary unity of God's design.

Evolution of life, hominization, then divinization, are one and the same movement of God who gives and draws life towards the universal focus, the three eternal persons who move the universe without ever being confused with it.

At the heart of the world in genesis are the Three Persons, Source of Being, Principal of Creative Evolution and Goal of the prodigious history of the cosmos, humanized and soon transfigured.

This is what St John tells us in his vision.

Then I saw a new heaven and a new earth;
for the first heaven and the first earth had passed
*   away,*
and the sea was no more (Rev. 21.1).

The dwelling of God is with men.
He will dwell with them,
and they shall be his people,
and God himself will be with them;
he will wipe away every tear from their eyes,
and death shall be no more,
neither shall there be mourning nor crying nor pain
*   any more,*
for the former things have passed away (Rev.
21.3-4).

Prayer to Christ, always Greater .

Lord of consistence and union, you whose *distinguishing mark* and *essence* is the power indefinitely to grow greater, without distortion or loss of continuity, to the measure of the mysterious Matter whose Heart you fill and all whose movements you ultimately control – Lord of my childhood and Lord of my last days – God, complete in relation to yourself and yet, for us, continually being born – God, who, because you offer yourself to our worship as 'evolver' and 'evolving' are henceforth the only being that can satisfy us – sweep away at last the clouds that still hide you – the clouds of hostile prejudice and those, too, of false creeds.

Let your universal Presence spring forth in a blaze that is at once Diaphany and Fire.

O ever-greater Christ!

Pierre Teilhard de Chardin, *The Heart of Matter*,
pp.57f.

Contemplation of this new world should lead us to this hymn of praise:

Worthy art thou, our Lord and God,
to receive glory and honour and power,
for thou didst create all things,
and by thy will they existed and were created (Rev.
4.11).

For Further Reading

Introduction

Ian G. Barbour, *Issues in Science and Religion*, Prentice-Hall and SCM Press 1966, reissued Harper Torchbooks 1971
Don Cupitt, *The Worlds of Science and Religion*, Sheldon Press 1976
S. L. Jaki, *Science and Creation*, Scottish Academic Press 1974
Russell Stannard, *Science and the Renewal of Belief*, SCM Press 1982

Chapter 1

D. J. Bartholomew, *God of Chance*, SCM Press 1984
Alister Hardy, Robert Harvey and Arthur Koestler, *The Challenge of Chance*, Hutchinson 1973
J. Lewis (ed), *Beyond Chance and Necessity*, Garnstone Press 1974
Jacques Monod, *Chance and Necessity*, Collins 1972
Hugh Montefiore, *The Probability of God*, SCM Press 1985
James D. Watson, *The Double Helix*, Penguin Books 1970

Chapter 2

Charles Darwin, *The Origin of Species*, Penguin Books 1970
Alister Hardy, *The Living Stream*, Collins 1965
Alister Hardy, *The Divine Flame*, Collins 1966
Julian Huxley, *Evolution*, Allen and Unwin 1974
Alan Moorehead, *Darwin and the 'Beagle'*, Penguin Books 1971
A. R. Peacocke, *Creation and the World of Science*, OUP 1979

Chapter 3

K. Lorenz, *Evolution and Modification of Behaviour*, Methuen 1966
Michael Polanyi, *Personal Knowledge*, Routledge 1973
I. T. Ramsey, *Biology and Personality*, Oxford University Press 1965
Gerd Theissen, *Biblical Faith*, SCM Press 1984
E. O. Wilson, *Sociobiology. The New Synthesis*, Harvard University Press 1980

Chapter 4

Alister Hardy, *Darwin and the Spirit of Man*, Collins 1984
David E. Jenkins, *What is Man?*, SCM Press 1970

Richard E. Leakey, *The Making of Mankind*, Michael Joseph 1981
Karl R. Popper, *Objective Knowledge*, Oxford University Press 1972
Vernon Sproxton, *Teilhard de Chardin*, SCM Press 1971
Pierre Teilhard de Chardin, *Man's Place in Nature*, Fount Books 1970
Pierre Teilhard de Chardin, *The Phenomenon of Man*, Fount Books 1965
C. H. Waddington, *The Ethical Animal*, Allen and Unwin 1960

Chapters 5 and 6

Etienne Charpentier, *How to Read the Old Testament*, SCM Press 1982
Etienne Charpentier, *Howe to Read the New Testament*, SCM Press 1982
F. W. Dillistone, *The Christian Understanding of Atonement*, SCM Press 1984
John Hick, *Evil and the God of Love*, Fount Books 1968
L. Köhler, *Hebrew Man*, SCM Press 1973
Philip Toynbee, *Towards the Holy Spirit*, SCM Press 1973
H. W. Wolff, *Anthropology of the Old Testament*, SCM Press 1974

Chapter 7

David E. Jenkins, *The Glory of Man*, SCM Press 1967
Hugh Montefiore (ed), *Man and Nature*, Collins 1975
Pierre Teilhard de Chardin, *Le Milieu Divin*, Fount Books 1969
Pierre Teilhard de Chardin, *The Future of Man*, Fount Books 1969

Conclusion

A. R. Peacocke (ed), *The Sciences and Theology in the Twentieth Century*, Oriel Press 1981
Pierre Teilhard de Chardin, *Hymn of the Universe*, Fount Books 1969
Pierre Teilhard de Chardin, *Science and Christ*, Collins 1968
Pierre Teilhard de Chardin, *The Heart of Matter*, Collins 1977